Y0-CQK-087

Sniffy
THE VIRTUAL RAT
Version 4.5 for Windows

Lester Krames
Jeff Graham
Tom Alloway

Erindale College
University of Toronto

Brooks/Cole Publishing Company

I(T)P ™ An International Thomson Publishing Company

Pacific Grove • Albany • Bonn • Boston • Cincinnati • Detroit • London • Madrid • Melbourne
Mexico City • New York • Paris • San Francisco • Singapore • Tokyo • Toronto • Washington

Sponsoring Editor: *Marianne Taflinger*
Marketing Team: *Adrian Perenon* and *Margaret Parks*
Editorial Assistant: *Laura Donahue*
Production Coordinator: *Marlene Thom*
Manuscript Editor: *Harriet Serenkin*

Cover Design: *Vernon T. Boes*
Cover Illustration: *Harry Briggs*
Typesetting: *Scratchgravel Publishing Services*
Printing and Binding: *Malloy Lithographing, Inc.*

For more information, contact:

BROOKS/COLE PUBLISHING COMPANY
511 Forest Lodge Road
Pacific Grove, CA 93950
USA

International Thomson Editores
Campos Eliseos 385, Piso 7
Col. Polanco
11560 México D. F. México

International Thomson Publishing Europe
Berkshire House 168–173
High Holborn
London WC1V 7AA
England

International Thomson Publishing GmbH
Königswinterer Strasse 418
53227 Bonn
Germany

Thomas Nelson Australia
102 Dodds Street
South Melbourne, 3205
Victoria, Australia

International Thomson Publishing Asia
221 Henderson Road
#05–10 Henderson Building
Singapore 0315

Nelson Canada
1120 Birchmount Road
Scarborough, Ontario
Canada M1K 5G4

International Thomson Publishing Japan
Hirakawacho Kyowa Building, 3F
2–2–1 Hirakawacho
Chiyoda-ku, Tokyo 102
Japan

Printed in the United States of America

10   9   8   7   6   5   4   3   2   1

Software License Notice
The software described herein is furnished under a license agreement. For single users
the license is printed at the back of the *User's Guide* and is an extension of this
copyright page. Network or site licenses must be executed separately. This software
may be used or copied only in accordance with the terms of the appropriate license.

Trademark Notice
Windows and Excel are registered trademarks of Microsoft Corporation. Apple, the
Apple logo, AppleLink, AppleShare, HyperCard, QuickTime, ResEdit, PowerPC, and
Macintosh are registered trademarks of Apple Computer, Inc. Sniffy is a trademark of
the Governing Council of the University of Toronto. Reference to these or other products
is for informational purposes only, and no endorsement or recommendation is implied.

How to Contact Brooks/Cole

General Inquiries:

U.S.A.
Brooks/Cole Publishing Company
511 Forest Lodge Road
Pacific Grove, CA 93950-5098

(408) 373-0728 (8:30 A.M.–5:00 P.M., Pacific Time)
(408) 375-6414 (FAX)
email: info@brookscole.com

Canada
Nelson-Canada
1120 Birchmount Rd.
Scarborough, Ontario
Canada M1K 5G4

(416) 752-9100
(416) 752-9812 (FAX)

Orders for Brooks/Cole Products (Books or Software):

International Thomson Publishing Distribution Center
7625 Empire Drive
Florence, KY 41042

Books: (800) 354-9706 (8:00 A.M.–5:00 P.M., Eastern Time)
Software: (800) 487-3575
(606) 525-0978 (FAX)

Technical Support for Brooks/Cole Software Customers:

International Thomson Publishing, Inc.
511 Forest Lodge Road
Pacific Grove, CA 93950-5098

(800) 327-0325 (6:00 A.M.–5:00 P.M., Pacific Time
                                9:00 A.M.–8:00 P.M., Eastern Time)
(408) 373-0351 (FAX)
e-mail: support@brookscole.com

This book is dedicated to the people close to us
whose love, devotion, and support helped sustain
our efforts through all the phases of this project:
Carol Krames, Janice Graham, and James Beckwith.

Contents

Preface

Sniffy the Virtual Rat is a popular, affordable computer program that enables students to explore the principles of shaping and partial reinforcement in operant conditioning, using a "virtual rat" named Sniffy. Each student learns by doing—conditioning his or her own "rat"—and experiences many of the benefits of animal experimentation but none of the drawbacks associated with using live animals.

Sniffy solves a number of ethical problems and financial constraints. Rather than using live animals to conduct research that is a replication of important historical studies, students experience firsthand operant conditioning with the virtual rat. Some people argue that research with live animals is justifiable only when there is a significant advance in theory and understanding, which would disallow using live animals for teaching at the undergraduate level. In addition, for many colleges and universities, the costs of maintaining an animal facility for undergraduate teaching are prohibitive. Sniffy offers an inexpensive alternative.

Students learn:

- *Observational techniques:* quantifying and summarizing the animal's behavior repertoire before training.
- *Magazine training:* training Sniffy to orient to the sound of food being delivered, so that the sound becomes a secondary reinforcer.
- *Shaping behavior:* conditioning Sniffy to press a bar in an operant chamber for food through a procedure involving successive approximation.
- *Reinforcement schedules:* exploring the effects of the four simple partial reinforcement schedules on the maintenance and extinction of bar-pressing behavior.
- *The cumulative recorder:* a response-measurement device that is used to record the rate of bar pressing and to indicate which responses were reinforced.

- *Conditioning:* observing the changes in Sniffy's behavior as he becomes conditioned. Each of Sniffy's 15 behavior patterns can be trained to occur more frequently in one of a dozen different locations in the operant chamber.
- *Extinction:* measuring the time of extinction when reinforcement is no longer delivered.

New Features in Version 4.5 and Improvements to Version 4.0

- *Spontaneous recovery:* observing the re-emergence of bar pressing after that behavior has been extinguished and Sniffy has been removed from the chamber for some time.
- *Simulation techniques:* learning about behavior modeling by varying the parameters of Sniffy's learning algorithms. A new Modeling Parameters menu allows the instructor to set a range of default values that students can test.
- *Animation quality:* setting display rate to optimize performance on any personal computer with a 386 processor or higher. In effect, this allows you to adjust how quickly Sniffy moves around the chamber.
- *Help facility:* browsing for operating suggestions and training hints.
- *Error checking and preference file:* new error messages warn users of suboptimal configurations, and a preference file (sniffy.ini) is now written to the Windows directory to save customized parameter settings.

Who Are the Users?

Sniffy is designed to teach undergraduate students about operant conditioning. It is useful for any student taking a beginning psychology course. We have also used Sniffy with elementary school children taking summer courses on our campus. Their enthusiasm for the "Sniffy game" is remarkable, considering that other computer games are also available. Other users of Sniffy include counselors and care-givers in situations where behavior is modified using reinforcement techniques. Sniffy serves well as an introduction to the principles of operant conditioning used in therapy.

One reviewer writes: "I believe this program can be of great value in courses on the psychology of learning, behavior analysis, and behavior modification. I have no doubt that one day students will learn to do behavior modification on a simulator just as today students learn to fly planes in simulators."

How Does Sniffy Improve Learning?

Instead of just reading about the laboratory procedures, students are able to experience firsthand the training of a "laboratory animal." Anecdotal evidence suggests that the interactive nature of the Sniffy program is appealing and effective. Some student comments are as follows:

> "Sniffy was a helpful and entertaining way to learn about operant conditioning. It taught us that it is more of a challenge than was expected, from looking at the utopian world of Walden Two, for example, to actually train a rat to simply press a bar."

> "I applaud the designers of Sniffy for making it so user friendly. I am almost completely computer-illiterate, and yet I accessed, used, and exited Sniffy with relative ease. I did not even have to beg for help from the lab staff."

> "We walked into the MacLab in the Psych shack and were confronted with howls of disappointment and a barrage of encouraging words. 'Come on, Sniffy! You can do it! Just a little further to the left. . . .' Needless to say we were a little skeptical over all the excitement. However, as soon as we turned on our copy of Sniffy 4.5, we found ourselves just as enthusiastic about our virtual rat."

Some reviewers' comments:

> "I found the simulation interesting and not too simple. In fact, I felt some satisfaction at finally teaching Sniffy to bar press. Students no doubt would feel the same way."

> "I'd have Sniffy projects that students would be required to submit (on disk). . . . I'd have contests: Who can magazine train a 'naive' Sniffy fastest? Who can maintain behavior on the thinnest schedule? Who can shape some new behavior fastest? Etc. I might actually make a shaping project part of the final exam."

Other comments address the obvious differences between Sniffy and a real rat, offering suggestions for improvement. We encourage you to send us your comments as well. A common concern we share with others is the need to make clear to students that, when it comes to gaining new insights, simulations can never replace research with real animals.

How Does an Instructor Teach with Sniffy?

The major features of operant conditioning can be taught in a couple of two-hour lab sessions. Typically, the first allows students to train Sniffy to press the bar for food, and the second explores the behavioral effects of various partial reinforcement (PRF) schedules. On the PRF schedules, the cumulative recorder displays a prototypic curve indicating the typical differences observed among the four simple schedules. However, the exact slope and shape of a real rat's training curve have not been replicated. Satiation, discrimination, and chaining are phenomena that have not yet been implemented in the current version of Sniffy but are planned for the future.

Using Sniffy in a Variety of Classes

This manual details step by step how to set up your software, run the prepared exercises, and design your own laboratory modules. The exercises in this manual barely scratch the surface of the simulation's capabilities. Many hours would be required to test the limits of Sniffy's behavior under PRF schedules, different shaping techniques, and spontaneous recovery conditions. Sniffy can be used in upper-level or graduate courses that explore modeling techniques or neural networks. The advanced user's guide in this manual (Chapter 4) provides the details required to modify the learning algorithms and test the behavioral changes that result.

Acknowledgments

The creators of Sniffy—Tom Alloway, Jeff Graham, Les Krames, and Greg Wilson—would like to thank all those involved in the Sniffy project since 1991.

Many friends have helped during the design and testing phases. Thanks are due to our animator Nick Woolridge and our testers Chris

England, Hubert Marczuk, Roc Scalera, Mike Hynes, Dave De Angelis, Mary Ribelo, Kim Nichol, Mira Jelic, Anne Dmitrovic, Sandra Chang, and Bill Meredith. We appreciate the technical and financial support we have received from Professor Doug Chute of Drexel University, Marianne Taflinger of Brooks/Cole Publishing Company, Apple Canada, and the University of Toronto.

We acknowledge the principal and deans of Erindale College and the Governing Council of the University of Toronto for their generous financial and collegial assistance in initiating and maintaining this undertaking. In appreciation we have donated all of our software royalties to the university to fund new computer equipment in our labs.

We also thank the thousands of students who have worked with Sniffy in our teaching lab, helping us to refine and improve the laboratory exercises that are provided in Chapter 3.

We thank the many reviewers of Sniffy 4.0, Sniffy 4.5, and Sniffy 4.5 for Windows for their questions, comments, and debugging help. We appreciate the time it takes to learn a new teaching application and to identify its weaknesses. We appreciate the helpful comments of the reviewers: Hank Cetola, Adrian College; Paul Chance, Salisbury State University; Brian C. Cronk, Missouri Western State College; Kathleen M. Galotti, Carleton College; Mark Garrison, Kentucky State University; William L. Heward, The Ohio State University; Lloyd Komatsu, Carleton College; Tim Lawson, College of Mount St. Joseph; Julie Neiworth, Carleton College; John Nichols, Tulsa Junior College; Jesse E. Purdy, Southwestern University; Randolph A. Smith, Ouachita Baptist University; Larry Upton, North Carolina State University; M. Lisa Valentino, Seminole Community College; and William U. Weiss, University of Evansville.

We are currently working on Sniffy 5.0 for Macintosh and Windows, improving the graphic realism and incorporating almost all the suggestions received from our reviewer pool. Thanks go to Roc, Tom, and Hubert for managing our production team, to Al Sura for plotting the path to our full-video Sniffy 5.0, and to James Beckwith for his assistance with the Windows help system.

Finally, Tom, Les, and Jeff would like to congratulate Greg Wilson on his creative programming skills that enabled him to build this project from the ground up on a Macintosh platform and convert it entirely to a Windows platform. Kudos, kid! . . . TUVA. . . .

0

Quick Start

This laboratory manual describes how to use Sniffy the Virtual Rat, a computer simulation of operant conditioning. The Sniffy program is designed to teach the principles of shaping and partial reinforcement in operant conditioning. Many other uses are possible, although some limitations should be noted. This simulation cannot exhibit discrimination learning, chaining, punishment, and many other conditioning phenomena. Suggestions for which features should receive priority in the next version would be appreciated. (Contact the authors by e-mail at LKRAMES or JGRAHAM@credit.erin.utoronto.ca. Or visit our Web page; contact info@brookscole.com for details.) Version 4.5 is an upgrade of version 4.0 (MacLaboratory Inc., 1993); it now includes spontaneous recovery after a time-out, water deprivation options, and other programming features that allow advanced users access to the learning algorithm.

We assume that you are familiar with the basic operation of Windows 3.1.x or Windows 95. If not, you will need to ask your instructor for help and/or read your computer user's guide.

System Requirements, Installation, and Technical Support

Your Sniffy will run best on a computer with a 386 (or higher) processor running Windows 3.1.x or Windows 95. Extensive testing was done on a variety of 386, 486, and Pentium-based computers with 14" color VGA and SVGA monitors. The software has run under OS2 Warp, although it is not guaranteed to work and therefore that operating system is not currently supported. The ITP Technical Support Group is prepared to support Sniffy 4.5 under the Windows 3.1.x and Windows 95 operating systems. Sniffy can be run over a network, installed on each computer's hard disk, or run off a disk. Students will, in most cases, be running their own Sniffy program and saving their experiments on their disks.

Memory requirements for Sniffy depend on the specific computer configuration used. Some configurations require as little as 1.5 MB of available memory; other configurations with very high resolution monitors may require 5 MB or more of memory. Sniffy requires this extra memory to ensure the speed of animation is acceptable. If your are unable to launch Sniffy or Sniffy runs out of memory, we recommend you increase the size of virtual memory available to Windows.

Sniffy is shipped on a high-density 1.4 MB disk, accompanied by a help utility and example training files. When Sniffy is installed it will reside in the C:\sniffy directory, which will also contain C:\sniffy\help and C:\sniffy\examples subdirectories.

To install the software:
1. Place the disk into drive A:.
2. Select the A:\ drive window in the File Manager (Windows 3.1.x), or double-click 3½ inch floppy (A:) in **my computer** (Windows 95).
3. Double-click setup.exe (or the setup icon in Windows 95).

The installer builds a Sniffy the Virtual Rat program group, adds the necessary directories to your C:\ hard drive, and installs the help system and readme files. In your program group you will see icons for the Sniffy program, Help and readme files, and eight example files.

To start the program in Windows 3.1.x, open the Sniffy the Virtual Rat program group and double-click the Sniffy icon as illustrated in Figure 0.1. To start the program in Windows 95, click the Start button, select Programs, then select Sniffy the Virtual Rat, and finally select Sniffy.

In some situations students will prefer to run directly off their disk (for example, on locked networks). To do so they will have to install their software on their home machine and copy the sniffy.exe file and both the Help and Examples directories to the run-time disk. To ensure sufficient space on the disk for their own work, students will have to delete some of the example files.

To run Sniffy off your disk:
1. Place the run-time disk into drive A:.
2. Select the A:\ drive window in the File Manager (Windows 3.1.x), or double-click 3½ inch floppy (A:) in **my computer** (Windows 95).
3. Double-click sniffy.exe (or the Sniffy icon in Windows 95).

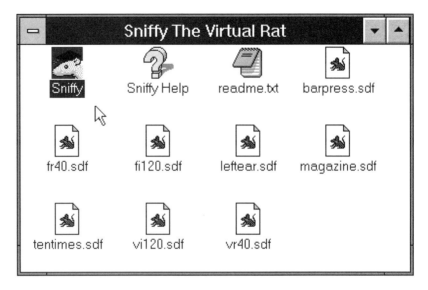

Figure 0.1

You can save an experiment file so that when that file is opened again, Sniffy will have retained what he learned. On-line help is available under the Help menu when the program is running. Changes to any modeling parameter values are automatically stored in a preference file called sniffy.ini inside the Windows directory. Please make sure you keep a safe copy of the original files, and make all changes on secondary copies.

Sniffy the Virtual Rat was designed by

Tom Alloway, Jeff Graham, Les Krames, and Greg Wilson
Department of Psychology, Erindale College
University of Toronto
3359 Mississauga Rd.
Mississauga, Ontario L5L1C6
telephone: (905) 569-4303
        fax: (905) 569-4326
    e-mail: jgraham@credit.erin.utoronto.ca
        or: antguy@io.org
        or: lkrames@credit.erin.utoronto.ca

See our Sniffy the Virtual Rat Web page on the World Wide Web. Contact our support line at info@brookscole.com for access information.

What Do You Get?

When you open the Sniffy the Virtual Rat program group installed on your hard disk, you will find 11 items: the Sniffy application, a Sniffy help system, a readme.txt file, and eight example training files saved at various points in training.

The Help file can be read from within the program by using the Help menu or by double-clicking the yellow question mark icon in the Sniffy the Virtual Rat program group. Most of the contents of this file are presented in Chapter 2 and should be read by all owners of Sniffy for details about the system setup requirements and the installation procedures.

When Sniffy has successfully launched, you will see two windows as shown in Figure 0.2. The top window is the operant chamber, and the bottom window is the cumulative record that records Sniffy's bar presses and food reinforcements. Both windows can be moved by selecting and dragging their title bars.

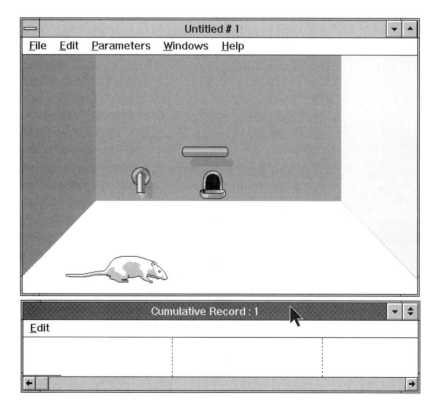

Figure 0.2

If your computer is running too slowly, Sniffy may exhibit abnormal behavior on some reinforcement schedules. After the program is started, it will warn you once with the display shown in Figure 0.3 if this is the case. The first fix is to select the Parameters menu while holding the shift key down, then select Modeling Parameters..., and set the Animation Governor to "fast." You can ignore this "too slow" warning if it is shown when you have the Help window or other dialog boxes open for some period of time. If Sniffy still runs into trouble launching, you can change the amount of memory allocated to Windows.

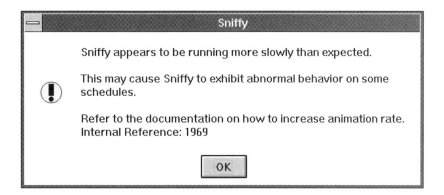

Figure 0.3

When the Sniffy software is started, you will wait a few seconds while the components of the program are being loaded. At long last, Sniffy is beamed in. (A real rat would be gently placed in the middle of the operant chamber.) As Sniffy wanders around the training box, your task begins.

Chapter 1 provides an introduction to operant conditioning and behavioral psychology. Chapter 2 offers a detailed explanation of the operating interface and menu features as well as a summary of the main procedures the trainer needs to use.

For now, the only hint we will give is that when you click the lever on the back wall or press the spacebar on the keyboard, a food pellet drops into the food hopper. (If the hopper is full, a second food pellet cannot be delivered. An attempt to do so should generate a different sound. If you don't hear a different sound, check that the Default Beep and the Critical Stop events have been assigned different sounds in the Sound Control Panel.) Several training (that is, conditioning) exercises are provided in Chapter 3. Chapter 4 is a technical summary (advanced user's guide) for those who want to tinker with the performance of the simulation and play with the learning parameters that

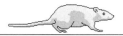

govern Sniffy's behavior. We hope you find this program an interesting challenge. Please feel free to send us a summary of the results of your explorations.

We do not warrant the suitability of Sniffy in any way. Please ensure that you have read and understand the provisions of the licensing agreement that you accept if you use this software.

1

Introduction to Operant Conditioning

The history of psychology is a struggle to deal with three main issues. The first issue concerns how information from the outside world gets inside our heads. Seeing, hearing, or any sensory experience is a translation of the physical world that surrounds us. The question of how this translation takes place gave rise to the field of perception.

The second question that psychologists ask is: Following the perception and processing of information, how is it stored? We are not passive "cameras" sensing the world around us. We further process the information that comes into our heads before storing it. As a result, the perception of environmental information has the potential to change us. These questions lead to the study of learning and memory.

The third question deals with how we determine what goals to seek. This last question gives rise to the field of motivation.

This manual deals with a small part of the second question, learning. Despite a long history of study, we still have a problem defining what we mean by learning. The problem is that we recognize that learning is basically a process that occurs somewhere in the body. The neuroscientist tries to explain learning in terms of changes in synapses between neurons, but these changes are difficult to localize or observe.

How do we deal with this problem? Psychology can be defined as the scientific study of behavior, and the psychologist views learning as a behavioral phenomenon. Observation of behavior is the principal tool used by psychologists to make inferences about underlying processes. Few of the phenomena studied by psychologists are directly observable. Even a phenomenon as obvious as development must be studied through inference. We could watch an infant from the time of birth until age one and try to describe the development. However, the changes are so gradual that they are difficult to observe. It is not an unusual experience for a parent to meet friends who comment how

much their child has grown. It often takes such remarks for the parents to stop and notice the child's development.

How then do we study psychological phenomena? To use the above example, we might study the behaviors of a group of newborn infants and compare their behaviors with those of a group of one-year-olds. The difference in the behaviors of the two groups could be ascribed to development.

From this example, we see that, although behavior is the subject matter of psychology, our ability to make inferences often comes from observing changes in behavior. Take another interesting example. Your instructor has the task of assigning grades to each member of your class. The fairest method of making these assignments might be to give grades according to how much each student has learned. The students who have learned the most would get the highest grades. But how do you assess who learned what?

One solution might be to require all members of the class to undergo exploratory brain surgery at the beginning of the term. During the operation, the instructor could examine and count the connections between the neurons in each student's brain. Then your instructor would sew you back together, give the course, and repeat the surgery at the end of the term. Finally, the students with the most new neural connections would receive the highest grades.

There are two problems with this approach. First, the enrollment in the course would be very low. Second, even if we looked in each student's brain, we would not know where to look and which neural connections to count.

How then do we assign grades? We start with the simple assumption that if you took the final exam on the first day of class, you would fail. The hypothetical change in behavior from failing at the beginning of the year to passing after completion of the course is what we ascribe to learning. Thus, we assume that marks on tests and examinations that assess knowledge of course material reflect how much students have learned.

Definition of Learning

The definition of learning that we will use reflects the problems that we have noted and points to some of the solutions. *We define learning as a psychological process inferred from observations of relatively permanent changes in behavior that occur as a result of practice.* We have

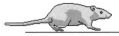

already seen why learning is a process that must be observed from changes in behavior. The rest of the definition helps us distinguish between changes in behavior that we want to be able to ascribe to learning and behavior changes that can more reasonably be ascribed to other inferred processes.

Saying that learning produces relatively *permanent* changes in behavior helps us distinguish between changes in behavior that we want to ascribe to learning and changes in behavior that are better ascribed to changes in motivation. Suppose that we trained a food-deprived rat to obtain food by running through a complex maze with many blind alleys. Over many trials, the number of blind alleys that the rat enters on its way to the goal chamber and the amount of time that the rat requires to get there would both decrease; we would like to say that these behavior changes are due to learning. However, the rat's running speed can be manipulated easily by increasing or decreasing the amount of food offered in the goal chamber of the maze. If we increase the amount of food, the rat will run faster; if we decrease the amount of food, the rat will run slower. Moreover, these changes occur quickly from one trial to the next. Most psychologists would say that these sudden, reversible changes result from changes in the rat's motivation. In a similar way, saying that learned changes in behavior must be the result of *practice* helps us distinguish changes in behavior due to learning from changes in behavior due to processes such as maturation, injury, and disease that also produce long-term behavior change.

The History of the Study of Learning

Ivan Pavlov was a Russian scientist who first became well known for his work on the physiology of digestion in dogs. During the first years of the twentieth century, Pavlov undertook a series of investigations that he hoped would clarify the role of saliva in digestion. He operated on the animals that were to be used in these studies, turning the salivary gland located in one of the dogs' cheeks around so that, instead of flowing into the dog's mouth, the saliva flowed to the outside where it was easier to collect and measure. Pavlov's objective was to determine whether the kind of food placed in his dogs' mouths affected the amount and the chemical composition of saliva.

However, Pavlov's experiments with salivation did not work out as planned. His experimental plan was based on the assumption that the

dogs would salivate only after food had been placed in their mouths. However, after only one day's experience with the experimental set-up, the dogs began to salivate while the tube used to collect the saliva was being attached; and after a few days, the animals began to salivate when Pavlov's technician came to remove them from their home cages. A less perceptive scientist might have abandoned these experiments that were not working out as planned. However, Pavlov recognized that this anticipatory salivation, which occurred when the hungry dogs were exposed to stimuli that had previously been associated with food, provided an objective way to measure the acquisition of learned associations. As a result, Pavlov undertook a series of systematic investigations of what has come to be called *classical conditioning*, and today Pavlov is more often remembered for his work on learning than for the studies of digestion for which he won the Nobel Prize for physiology in 1904.

Pavlov's work showed an important part of the learning picture but still left a number of unanswered questions. Edward Thorndike's research helped us understand how organisms learn what behaviors to perform in different situations. Thorndike, impressed by William James's classic textbook, *Principles of Psychology*, enrolled in Harvard and took courses with James. While at Harvard, Thorndike began the first experimental study of learning in animals. At the time, there was no formal psychological laboratory at Harvard, nor was there much financial support for his early work. Thus, James's home was his first laboratory.

Thorndike published his classic text *Animal Intelligence* in 1898, in which he described his first learning experiments. In these first experiments, Thorndike studied the way cats learn to escape from an apparatus that he called the *puzzle box*. The cats had to learn how to manipulate different levers to open the box so that they could escape. Initially, the cats emitted many different behaviors, most of which did not lead to escape. However, gradually by trial and error, the cats found the behaviors that led to escape. Thorndike recorded how long it took each cat to escape on each trial and found that the average time gradually decreased from several minutes to a few seconds. As the escape speeds increased, the subjects were learning to eliminate useless behaviors, while retaining the much smaller number of successful behaviors. The form of learning that Thorndike studied is often called *instrumental conditioning* because the animal's behavior is the "instrument" that it learns to employ in order to obtain something that it is motivated to get or get away from.

Thorndike asked the next obvious question: What is the reinforcing mechanism that strengthens and selects successful behaviors? The answer for Thorndike was the *Law of Effect*, which he stated as follows:

> Of several responses made to the same situation, those which are accompanied or closely followed by satisfaction to the animal will, other things being equal, be more firmly connected with the situation, so that, when it recurs, they will be more likely to recur; those which are accompanied or closely followed by discomfort to the animal will, other things being equal, have their connections with that situation weakened, so that, when it recurs, they will be less likely to occur. The greater the satisfaction or discomfort, the greater the strengthening or weakening of the bond. (cited by Kimble, 1961, p. 10)

Thorndike's experiments showed that the effect—the consequences—of a behavior determines whether instrumental conditioning will occur. Hitting the right combination of levers in Thorndike's puzzle box had the positive effect of opening the door and allowing the cat to escape. As is the case with most pioneers, Thorndike's models of instrumental conditioning and his statement of the Law of Effect have been subject to many modifications. However, they still stand as an important cornerstone of our understanding of the learning process.

B. F. Skinner

B. F. Skinner is the psychologist whose research helped to formulate the methods and procedures that describe a variant of Thorndike's instrumental conditioning that Skinner called *operant conditioning.* In Thorndike's work with puzzle boxes and subsequently in his studies of animals learning to run mazes, the learning tasks involved apparatus and procedures in which the animals had the opportunity to make a correct response only at certain well-defined times called *trials.* Skinner developed a learning situation in which an animal is confined during training in a cage called an *operant chamber*, which contains a device on which responses can be made as well as a mechanism, called the *magazine*, for the delivery of food. In an operant chamber, animals are trained in an experimental situation in which the opportunity to perform some response is continuously available. However, Skinner, like Thorndike, was interested in how the consequences of different

behavior patterns influence the likelihood or frequency with which the behaviors are repeated. Thus, we can view Skinner's work with operant conditioning as an extension of Thorndike's work with instrumental conditioning. Moreover, fundamentally the same principles of learning appear to apply both when the animal has the opportunity to make a correct response only at certain times, as in Thorndike's puzzle boxes and mazes, and when the animal is able to respond at any time, as in Skinner's operant chamber.

Skinner made three fundamental assumptions about behavior. First, animals are frequently active, a fact that means that organisms are continually *emitting* various behaviors. Second, these emitted behaviors frequently have consequences that influence the likelihood of their repetition in the future. Third, the effects of the consequences are influenced by the animal's motivational state as well as by the physical and social environment. For example, the effect of presenting food as a consequence for performing some behavior will depend on whether the animal has been deprived of food.

To understand Skinner's contribution to the psychology of learning, we need to examine what he called his form of *radical behaviorism*. Almost as much as Skinner's experimental work has influenced modern psychology, his attempt to create a philosophical framework has generated excitement and controversy. Skinner's radical behaviorism not only called for the objective study of behavior, it posited that behavior is often caused by events in the environment that can be discovered and manipulated to control the behavior. Thus, Skinner and many of his followers have been interested in practical applications of their work.

Another aspect of Skinner's radical behaviorism was his assertion that feelings, thoughts, emotions, and most other mental events should also be viewed as analogous to more readily observable emitted behaviors, rather than as causes of behavior. Of all of Skinner's propositions, this notion was perhaps the hardest for other psychologists and philosophers of science to accept. Intuitively, most people prefer to believe that actions are attributable to feelings and thoughts.

Skinner held that behavior is lawful. Although he recognized that behavior is jointly determined by the interaction of genetic and environmental factors, Skinner and his followers have concerned themselves almost exclusively with environmental effects. The historical reasons for this emphasis on the environment are complex, but one important reason is that environmental factors are easier to manipulate than genetic factors, especially in human beings where genetic ma-

nipulations are considered to be unethical. For example, a child's genes and the environment in which the child grows up jointly determine how tall the child will grow to be. However, while nothing can be done about a child's tallness genes once the embryo has been conceived, the diet that the child eats—an environmental factor—can significantly affect eventual adult height.

Skinner stated that psychologists should be concerned with discovering the laws of behavior and emphasized the importance of relating environmental causes to behavioral effects. However, he believed that it is often possible to discover behavioral laws without necessarily understanding what goes on inside the organism. He often used the metaphor of a black box to represent the individual. The box is opaque. The inside is not only invisible, we don't need to know what is going on inside to understand the rules of its behavior and control its actions. In fact, Skinner believed that trying to understand what goes on inside the box is sometimes confusing and misleading.

We can understand the point that Skinner was making by considering the common television set. Although few of us can produce or understand a circuit diagram of the inside of a television set, we can still operate one. We know that we must plug the set into an energy source. We know that, when we manipulate the channel selector, the stations change. We know that a second control adjusts the volume, while other controls make the picture flip and change the colors. The picture is the behavior of the set that we want to be able to predict and control, and we can control this behavior by altering the controls. If the set is not working properly, we also know that sometimes a sharp rap on the side of the box produces a better picture. None of this knowledge about how to control the behavior of a television set requires an understanding of its internal workings. Skinner believed that we can predict and control the behavior of organisms, including ourselves, in a similar way without necessarily understanding the internal workings of the body.

According to Skinner, psychologists should seek to discover relationships between the environment and behavior. Other kinds of scientists concern themselves with studying what goes on inside the black box, and their contributions are also valuable. But Skinner maintained that studying the relationship between behavior and environment is the exclusive domain of the psychologist.

Skinner proposed that the best way to study this relationship is to manipulate specific environmental events and measure the behavioral outcomes that result. Operant conditioning is a body of scientific procedures and findings that describe how interactions with environmental

stimuli can lead to changes in the frequency with which various behaviors are performed. The goal is the ability to control behavior through control of the environment.

Pavlov studied very simple behaviors that can be reliably elicited in all normal members of a species by presenting certain very specific stimuli. For example, food placed in a food-deprived dog's mouth will always elicit salivation; and a puff of air blown into a human's eye will always elicit an eye blink. Skinner studied more complex behaviors that organisms emit. The difference between elicited and emitted behaviors is that typically no single stimulus exists that will reliably produce these more complex behaviors. For example, there is no stimulus that will elicit grooming behavior or barking from all normal dogs in a fashion analogous to the way food in the mouth elicits salivation.

In fact, most behaviors that psychologists are interested in predicting and controlling are emitted, not elicited. Consider the behavior of students in class. Students not only listen to the instructor and take notes, they also scratch, yawn, read newspapers, shift around in their seats, and exhibit a wealth of other behaviors, almost all of which are emitted in the sense that no single stimulus exists whose presentation will reliably produce these behaviors in everyone.

The scientific question to which Skinner sought experimental answers was: How can we predict and control emitted behaviors? To address this question, Skinner developed the operant chamber, a very simple environment in which, according to Skinner, it is possible to discover how the environment determines the frequency with which animals and people produce emitted behaviors.

The Operant Conditioning Chamber: Sniffy's Classroom

Let's meet Sniffy, your virtual laboratory rat. Sniffy is a computer simulation of a rat in an operant chamber. He performs many of the behaviors you would see in a real rat, but his behavioral repertoire is more limited. For example, Sniffy is always hungry and ready to work for food no matter how much he has eaten.

Sniffy's operant chamber—which closely resembles those found in laboratories where psychologists do research on operant conditioning—provides a carefully controlled and simplified environment. A look at Sniffy's operant chamber reveals three objects on the back wall: a lever or so-called *bar* that you will train Sniffy to press, a water

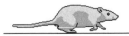

spout, and a food hopper (see Figure 0.2 on page 4). As in all operant conditioning situations, the bar is continuously available for Sniffy to press. The hopper is the device that you will use to provide a positive consequence or *reinforcement* when Sniffy does something that you want him to do more often. At the appropriate time, you will drop food into the hopper by pressing any key on your computer keyboard.

In this kind of limited environment, a real rat performs a limited subset of species-typical rat behaviors. As would be the case with a real rat, you can expect to see Sniffy rearing up, grooming himself, scratching, wandering around, and exploring the chamber. The experimenter can observe and record various behaviors in this chamber. The response most often chosen to record is bar pressing.

Reinforcement

Skinner described *reinforcement* as a procedure that makes a behavior pattern, or *response*, more likely to be repeated under similar circumstances in the future. In operant conditioning, the term *reinforcement* refers to the procedure of presenting or removing a stimulus (called a *reinforcer*) as a consequence for the performance of some behavior. A *positive reinforcer* is a stimulus that an animal will work to get, and the term *positive reinforcement* refers to the procedure of presenting a positive reinforcer as a consequence of a behavior pattern. You will use food as a positive reinforcer to train Sniffy in the operant chamber. You will give Sniffy pellets of food to get him to press the bar or do other things that you want him to do more often. A *negative reinforcer* is a stimulus that an animal will work to get away from, and the term *negative reinforcement* refers to the procedure of removing a negative reinforcer as a consequence of a behavior. Both positive and negative reinforcement have the effect of increasing the rate (the number of times per minute or hour) at which the reinforced operant response will occur under similar circumstances in the future.

Skinner decried the fact that much of our society is controlled by negative reinforcement. When we have a noisy next-door neighbor, we often bang on the wall to make the noise stop. Termination of the annoyance is negative reinforcement for wall banging under similar circumstances in the future. Children do homework to avoid parental nagging, a wife goes to visit her mother to escape her husband's abusive anger, a worker shows up for work on time in a strongly disliked

job to avoid unemployment. Skinner felt that such heavy reliance on negative reinforcement is a sign of a poorly planned society. He wrote several books and articles describing how society might be better organized based on knowledge of operant principles and extensive use of positive reinforcement.

Operant conditioning also defines two procedures for punishing behavior. Punishment is the mirror image of reinforcement. Whereas reinforcement causes operant behaviors to be repeated more often in the future, punishment causes behaviors to occur less often. A *positive punisher* is a stimulus whose presentation following the occurrence of some response makes that response occur less often in the future, and *positive punishment* is the name of the procedure involved in presenting a positive punisher. If you hit your puppy with a rolled-up newspaper and rub its nose in what it has done after it has a toilet accident in the house, you are employing positive punishment. A *negative punisher* is a stimulus whose removal following a response causes that response to occur less often in the future, and *negative punishment* is the procedure involved in removing a negative punisher to make a behavior occur less often. If your daughter misbehaves while watching her favorite television program and you send her to her room (thereby removing the negative punisher of access to a television program that she likes), you are employing negative punishment.

Note that the terms *negative* and *positive* have the same meaning when applied to punishment that they have when applied to reinforcement. Both positive reinforcers and positive punishers have their effects respectively of strengthening or weakening behaviors when you apply the stimuli or turn them on following a behavior pattern, and both negative reinforcers and negative punishers have their respective effects when the stimuli are removed or terminated. But remember: Both positive and negative reinforcement cause behaviors to occur more often, whereas both positive and negative punishment cause behaviors to occur less often.

In operant conditioning, subjects learn which behaviors produce which reinforcers or punishers in which situations. In more technical terms, psychologists often say that *operant conditioning involves learning a three-way contingency between a situation, a response, and reinforcing or punishing consequence.* However you say it, the effect of reinforcement is to select for the reinforced behavior at the expense of other non-reinforced behaviors. In other words, the effect of reinforcement is to make the reinforced behavior occur more often; and a side effect of reinforcement is that many non-reinforced behaviors occur less often because the subject comes to perform the reinforced behavior

so often that it has less time left to do other things. The effect of punishment is just the opposite of that of reinforcement. Punishment selects against the punished behavior, thereby making it occur less often and, as a side effect, making other non-punished behaviors occur somewhat more often. An animal's behavioral repertoire is a list of all the behaviors that the animal would ever perform. The effect of operant conditioning is always to modify the relative frequencies with which different behaviors in the behavioral repertoire occur.

Skinner argued that punishment, in either of its forms, is inappropriate for five basic reasons. First, unless the punishment is severe or frequently repeated, its effect is only temporary. For example, if you yell at your cat whenever you see it jump up on the furniture, what you can expect to happen is that the behavior will stop as long as you are around, but the cat will continue to jump up on the furniture when you are not there. The cat will learn which reinforcers and punishers are associated with the behavior in which situations. In the situation when you are there, the cat will stay off the furniture as a result of your repeated mild punishment. In the situation when you are not there, the cat will jump up on the furniture if doing so produces some kind of reinforcement such as escape from a cold draft or the opportunity to watch birds outside the window. Another example of punishment's ineffectiveness can be seen every day on the highway. A police officer is a punishing agent. If we speed, we risk getting a ticket that costs us time, money, and possibly a license suspension. On the highway in the presence of a police car, drivers are scrupulous about their driving. Nobody tailgates, nobody speeds, everybody signals lane changes. When the police car exits the highway, illegal behaviors reappear.

Second, although punishment may suppress certain unwanted behaviors, it sometimes causes other undesirable behaviors. If you yell at your cat too often, it may become afraid of you and hide whenever you are around.

Third, punishment often elicits unwanted emotional responses. The punished individual may feel guilt, shame, fear, or rage. Otherwise reasonable, law-abiding citizens frequently become abusive when a police officer hands them a traffic ticket. A punished student may associate the shame of punishment with the classroom and drop out of school.

Fourth, punishment is a much less effective training tool than reinforcement because punishment provides so little information about what should be done. When you punish an animal or child for doing something, you are in effect telling the subject not to perform one particular item in its behavioral repertoire in the situation where the punishment occurred, but punishment provides no information about

which behaviors *are* appropriate in that situation. Reinforcement is a much more powerful training tool than punishment because reinforcement tells the animal or child what it should do.

Finally, perhaps the most serious problem with punishment is that it is habit-forming. We might wonder why punishment is used so much when so many problems are associated with it. The answer may seem paradoxical. Punishment works. It gives immediate results. In other words, punishment often provides negative reinforcement to the *person applying the punishment*. The displeasing behavior stops. The cat jumps down off the furniture when you yell at it. However, as Skinner reminds us, the solutions that we achieve with punishment are often short-term, and punishment has many undesirable side-effects.

Operant Conditioning: The Technique

Sniffy can already press the bar even before you train him to do so. What are we accomplishing when we condition Sniffy? We are taking a low-frequency or improbable behavior and causing it to occur much more often. When you condition Sniffy to press the bar, you are not teaching him to do something he was incapable of doing previously. What you are doing is increasing the frequency with which bar pressing occurs in the operant chamber. In fact, you can increase the frequency of *any* of Sniffy's behaviors by giving him a food pellet immediately after he performs the target behavior that you have selected. The food pellets are, of course, a positive reinforcer; by presenting one of them immediately after Sniffy does something that you want him to do more often, you will be using positive reinforcement to train him.

Training Sniffy will teach you the virtue of patience. You will learn what operant conditioners mean when they say ruefully that, when you place an animal in an environment where everything is under the experimenter's control, the animal will do exactly whatever it pleases. All the things that Sniffy does in the operant chamber are emitted behaviors. That fact means that you must wait until the ornery little beast finally performs the target behavior so that you can reinforce him. Such are the joys of life for a psychologist!

Since reinforcement is the only tool that you have, it's a good idea to know as much as possible about it. Knowing the effect of a behavioral consequence is another way of saying we know what motivates behavior. Water delivered to a hungry Sniffy will not lead to bar pressing. Typically, Skinner would bring his animals into the lab and monitor

their weight. Before the experiment, he would restrict their access to food and wait until the animals were at 80% of the normal body weight. This procedure motivated his animals to perform tasks where the reinforcer was food. You may assume that Sniffy is currently at 80% of his normal body weight and thus hungry.

To be effective, the reinforcer must be presented immediately after the target behavior has occurred. Suppose that you wanted to condition your roommate to clean up his share of the room. Complimenting him immediately after a clean-up and taking him out for a pizza just then would be much more effective than if you waited a week before praising him and buying him the pizza.

In the case of Sniffy learning to press a bar, immediacy of reinforcement is crucial. If there is a delay of even a second or two, instead of strengthening the target behavior, the delay will result in the reinforcer increasing the likelihood of whatever behavior Sniffy happens to be performing a second or two after he performs the target behavior. If the food arrives just as Sniffy is turning and walking away, then "turning and walking away" will be the reinforced behavior that will increase in frequency.

You might want to see how effectively you will be able to reinforce Sniffy in your experiment. Position the cursor over the bar and click the mouse button or press any key on the computer keyboard. Immediately you will see and hear food being dropped into the hopper. How long does it take Sniffy to find and eat the food? Unless Sniffy was very near the food hopper when the pellet dropped, he won't find the food immediately. This fact points to an important procedural problem.

The last thing that Sniffy did before eating the food pellet was poke his nose into the food hopper. What will the food pellet (the positive reinforcer) reinforce? We want to reinforce Sniffy for bar pressing, not poking his nose into the hopper. This means that we need a positive reinforcer that we can deliver immediately after Sniffy presses the bar.

Magazine Training: Sniffy Learns a Signal That Food Is Available

The first step in teaching Sniffy to press the bar is *magazine training*. Magazine training is a technique that involves using what amounts to a classical-conditioning procedure to turn an originally neutral stimulus into a *secondary reinforcer*. *Primary reinforcers* are stimuli whose reinforcing power is intrinsic in a properly motivated animal. Food serves as a reinforcer for a food-deprived rat and is a primary

reinforcer because its reinforcing power is intrinsic to the stimulus for a hungry rat.

A *secondary reinforcer* is a stimulus that has acquired reinforcing power as a result of being paired with a primary reinforcer. Nearly any stimulus that is not intrinsically a reinforcer can become a secondary reinforcer when paired with a primary reinforcer. *Magazine training* is the technical name for the procedure that you are going to use to turn the sound made by the food-delivery mechanism (the so-called *magazine*) into a secondary reinforcer for Sniffy.

Magazine training begins your interaction with Sniffy. What you will do depends on what Sniffy does, and what Sniffy does will depend on what you do. To begin, you wait until Sniffy is quite near the food hopper, and then you press any key on the keyboard. This will cause the magazine to drop a food pellet into the food hopper, making an audible clanking sound.

If Sniffy is close enough, he will find the food quickly and start to form an association between the sound and the presence of the food pellet. To save time, you may want to give Sniffy several pellets of food before he starts to wander off. Next, you can deliver the food pellets when he's a little farther away from the hopper. If you have given Sniffy enough pellets when he was quite close to the food hopper, he will orient to the hopper and go get the food pellet when he is somewhat farther away. Now you can let him wander a little farther away before giving him the next pellet, even farther away the next time, and so on.

Eventually you will be able to "call" Sniffy from any part of the chamber by operating the magazine. At this point, he is magazine trained, and the sound of the food-delivery mechanism has become a secondary reinforcer. Whenever you operate the food-delivery mechanism, Sniffy will be instantly reinforced for doing whatever he was doing just before he heard the sound. After hearing the sound, he will stop what he was doing and go eat the food pellet. The consumption of the food will maintain the secondary reinforcing power of the sound.

Shaping: Letting Sniffy Know What Behavior Makes Food Available

Sniffy has an extensive behavioral repertoire, and bar pressing is part of it, even before training. The operant chamber is programmed so that a pellet of food is dropped into the food hopper every time he presses the bar. Once he is magazine trained, Sniffy will learn to bar press all

by himself if you just leave him alone for an hour or so. Sniffy will eventually learn to bar press if he is simply placed in the chamber even without magazine training, but it takes much longer for him to train himself to bar press without magazine training. Of course, for most behaviors learned in natural situations, the animal has to "magazine train" itself—that is, it has to learn what stimuli signal the availability of food.

However, if you are observant and have a good sense of timing, you can speed up this learning process by using a technique called *shaping*. Shaping is the technical name of the procedure employed to train an animal to do often something that it normally does rarely (or not at all) by reinforcing successive approximations of the desired behavior. Shaping means that the experimenter (teacher) follows a procedure that leads the subject (learner) to progress by small steps. Reinforcement is made available for progress and then withheld until more progress is made.

Shaping involves accepting as a first criterion for reinforcement something that is less than the final target behavior but that somehow resembles the target behavior. For example, a parent who becomes excited about a child's first approximation of a word is often reinforcing the child for making a sound that no one else can recognize. The child may babble a sound that the parent thinks resembles the word *daddy*. Eventually, however, even the parent loses interest until the sound becomes "da." Then even aunts and uncles become excited and reinforce the child. Slowly reinforcement is withheld for "da," and the child must say "dada" and then "daddy."

To be a successful shaper, you have to be a careful and patient observer. Shaping works because behavior is variable. The idea is that you pick a behavior that the animal performs fairly often and that is similar in some way to the target behavior. Reinforcing the chosen behavior will cause Sniffy to begin performing that behavior more frequently. However, Sniffy's behavior is not a rigidly performed routine. You will notice a number of different variations. Eventually, Sniffy will perform a variant of the behavior that resembles the target behavior more closely. That variant then becomes your second approximation, and you require him to repeat that variant to obtain reinforcement. As the second approximation is performed more frequently, the animal will eventually emit another variant that resembles the target even more closely, and so on.

Shaping an animal takes patience, careful observation, and good timing. It is a skill that you learn with practice. Sniffy is easier to shape than a real rat partly because he never gets enough to eat and partly

because his behavioral repertoire is smaller than that of a real rat. Nevertheless, shaping Sniffy is difficult enough for you to get an idea of both the frustration and the feeling of eventual triumph that shaping an animal engenders.

As your first approximation to bar pressing, you might try reinforcing Sniffy for rearing up anywhere in the chamber. Next, require him to rear up against the back wall where the bar is located. Then gradually require him to rear up closer and closer to the bar. If your patience, observational skills, and timing are good, you should have Sniffy bar pressing frequently in 40 minutes or so. If you are unusually skillful, you can condition him in half that time. However, if you are inattentive or have bad timing, you might have been better off letting Sniffy learn to bar press on his own after magazine training.

As we have seen, what an animal can learn depends partly on what it can already do. However, although limitations in the computer simulation mean that Sniffy cannot be trained to perform completely novel behaviors like turning somersaults, shaping can be employed to train a real animal to do things which are physically possible but which an untrained animal might never do. For example, training a physically fit cat to stand or walk on its hind legs without support is a fairly straightforward process even though untrained cats rarely, if ever, do it.

Pet-food manufacturers produce several brands of bite-size cat treats in several flavors, and it is often possible to find some variety of cat treat that your cat likes so much that the animal will work to obtain them. In fact, the cat may like them so much that you'll have to keep the treats container locked away to prevent theft. Once you've found your cat's favorite, the treats will constitute a primary reinforcer that you can employ to teach your cat to stand and walk on its hind legs without support or to do other tricks.

As with Sniffy, the first step in training your cat will be magazine training. You need to find a stimulus that can be delivered with split-second timing when your cat does something right and that can be easily transformed into a secondary reinforcer by pairing it with treat presentation. Stores that sell party supplies often stock a variety of noise-making party favors for children's parties. What you need is a device that makes a nice clicking or popping sound.

You magazine train your cat in much the same way that you magazine train Sniffy. To begin, wait until your cat is near you. Then operate the noisemaker and give the cat a treat. After you have sounded the clicker and given the cat a treat a couple of times with the cat very close by, walk a short distance away before sounding the clicker and giving the cat the next treat. You will know your cat is well magazine

trained when you can call it from anywhere in the house just by making the noise.

Training a cat to stand on its hind legs involves progressively requiring the animal to get its head higher and higher off the ground before you reinforce it by sounding the noisemaker and giving it a treat. Start by watching the cat until by chance it lifts its head somewhat higher than usual. (Standing with the front paws up on something doesn't count.) Then sound the clicker and give the cat a treat. After several reinforcements, the cat will begin walking around with its head held high more often. Since the cat's behavior is variable, sooner or later it will raise its head higher than your first criterion level, and that new higher level then becomes your second approximation that the cat must match to get subsequent treats. By the time you have reached the third or fourth approximation, the cat will probably be sitting on its hind legs and lifting its front paws off the ground. If you are patient, you should be able to train the cat to stand on its hind legs and "beg" after only a few days of training.

If you decide to train your cat, you will discover that training a real animal is somewhat harder than training Sniffy. Part of the problem is that your cat has a larger behavior repertoire than Sniffy, and another part of the problem is that the cat is free to move about and approach you in a way that Sniffy isn't. One difficulty will almost certainly arise. During magazine training, when you start to move away from the cat, the cat will follow you. If you sit down with the treats and noisemaker in hand, the cat will jump into your lap. If you are standing up and walking around, the cat may jump on your shoulder. When these problems arise, don't punish the cat by yelling at or hitting it. You will greatly retard the learning process if you do anything to frighten the cat. However, if you never give the cat a treat unless you have first sounded the clicker, and if you never sound the clicker unless the cat is on the floor, the cat will learn to stay off you and "cooperate."

Another variant of operant conditioning that professional animal trainers use to teach animals to perform sequences of several distinct behaviors is called *backward chaining.* For example, suppose you wanted to train a rat to climb a ladder, walk across an elevated plank to a door, and open the door to obtain food. You would first train the rat to go through the open door to the food, then you would shape it to open the door to get access to the food. The next step would be to place the rat on the elevated platform at the top of the ladder so that it has to "walk the plank" to get to the door. Finally, you would shape ladder climbing to get to the platform. In other words, the idea of backward chaining is first to train the animal to do the last thing in the sequence

just before receiving the food. Then you make the opportunity to perform the last behavior in the sequence contingent on performing the next-to-last behavior, and so on. Most of the complex trained-animal performances that you see in a circus or zoo are achieved through a combination of shaping and backward chaining.

The Cumulative Recorder: Keeping Track of Sniffy's Progress

How do we know whether Sniffy has learned anything in the conditioning chamber? Remember that learning is a process that we infer as a result of a change in behavior. Sniffy can and does press the bar when he first enters the chamber, but he does so very seldom. Bar pressing becomes much more frequent after training. For this reason, Skinner chose simply to measure the frequency of occurrence of bar pressing; to make the necessary measurements, he invented the *cumulative recorder*. Skinner's cumulative recorder was a mechanical device that pulled a long roll of paper at a constant speed under a pen that rested on the surface of the moving paper. At the start, the pen was positioned at the bottom of the record; if the rat did not press the bar, the pen would simply draw a long straight horizontal line. However, every time the rat pressed the bar, the pen moved a notch upward toward the top of the paper. When the rat was pressing the bar, the resulting record was a sloping line that moved from the bottom edge toward the top of the record. The more often the rat pressed, the steeper the slope of line. In other words, Skinner's cumulative recorder drew a record in which the steepness of the line was directly proportional to the rate of bar pressing.

The roll of paper that Skinner used in his cumulative recorder was narrow; after recording a certain number of responses, the slanted line would eventually reach the top edge of the paper. When that happened, the pen very quickly reset to the bottom edge of the paper, causing a vertical line to be drawn across the paper from top to bottom. This pattern of a slanted line working its way to the top of the page followed by a sharp straight line to the bottom of the page gives a cumulative record the appearance of mountain peaks or waves.

In the Sniffy program, your computer will draw a cumulative record across the bottom part of the screen. These days, mechanical cumulative recorders of the sort that Skinner invented are rather obsolete. Scientists who study operant conditioning in research laboratories mostly use computers to draw cumulative records of bar pressing in a fashion

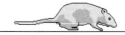

similar to the way the Sniffy program draws them. However, we have described the workings of Skinner's original mechanical device because we think that its operation is easier to understand than that of a computer program that simulates it.

The important thing for you to remember is that the slope of the rising lines on the graph represents the speed with which Sniffy is learning to press the bar. The steeper the slope, the more often Sniffy was pressing when the record was made. If Sniffy is pressing the bar seldom, it will take the slanted line some time to reach the top of the paper where the line resets to the bottom. This will result in a record that looks like gentle, undulating waves. If Sniffy is pressing often, the slanted line will reach the top faster, the pen will have to reset more often, and the resulting record will be more and steeper waves.

Conditioning: A New Behavior Takes Over

If you are a successful shaper, eventually Sniffy will press the bar four or five times within a minute. When that happens, just sit back and watch. Over the next several minutes, the response rate will climb; the cumulative record will become steeper and steeper. You will see that learning is (in part) a matter of changing the probability of occurrence of behaviors. Operant conditioning describes the technology for accomplishing these changes in animals and in people.

Extinction: What Happens When There Is No More Reinforcement?

Training of an operant behavior involves magazine training, shaping, and conditioning. Once Sniffy has been conditioned, we might wonder what would happen if we stopped reinforcing Sniffy's bar presses.

This sounds like a simple question, but it reflects some of the complexity of real-life learning situations that animals encounter. We have said that learning is relatively permanent. What happens if an animal learns to locate a food source, and that food source eventually disappears? If learning is permanent, does that mean that the animal has acquired learned behaviors that may subsequently risk exposing it to predators and other dangers even when there is very little chance of finding food? If learned behaviors are to be beneficial, they must also

be flexible enough to change to meet changing situations in the animal's environment.

Extinction is the technical name given to the events that occur when a previously learned behavior no longer leads to reinforcement. What will happen when Sniffy presses the bar and receives no food for his effort? After training Sniffy, you can turn off the food-delivery mechanism and observe what happens. You can do this by choosing the Training Schedule command from the Parameters menu. When you choose the Extinction option in the Training Schedule dialog box, observe what happens when bar pressing no longer produces food pellets. You can expect that Sniffy will continue to press the bar for some time, but the rate of his bar pressing will gradually decrease. Eventually the response rate will decline to the very low rate at which Sniffy pressed the bar prior to conditioning.

What is happening to produce this change in behavior? This time we are seeing a very probable behavior (bar pressing) become increasingly rarer. To understand what is going on, remember that changes in behavior constitute evidence for inferring that learning is occurring. Recall also that operant conditioning consists of learning which behaviors are followed by which reinforcers in which situations. Extinction is not a process of erasing or forgetting a previously learned behavior. Extinction is another example of a learned change in behavior. Originally Sniffy learned that bar presses were followed by the arrival of food pellets. During extinction, Sniffy learns that food pellets no longer appear when he presses the bar.

Spontaneous Recovery

We can see very clearly in another part of the Sniffy program that extinction is not a matter of unlearning or forgetting. Let's suppose we have conditioned Sniffy to press the bar for food and have permitted him to obtain a couple of hundred food pellets by pressing the bar. Next, let's suppose that we extinguished bar pressing by turning off the magazine so that Sniffy no longer is reinforced for bar pressing and then waiting long enough for his rate of bar pressing to decline to the same low level at which he pressed the bar prior to conditioning. So far our experiment is pretty much the same as what we described in the previous section. However, now we might wonder what would happen if we took Sniffy out of the operant chamber, returned him to

his home cage, and let him stay there for 24 hours before bringing him back to the operant chamber for a second extinction session. Will he go to the bar and start to press as he had previously been conditioned to do? Or will he just ignore the bar as he was doing at the end of his first extinction session?

What we would observe in this situation is that Sniffy would start pressing the bar more slowly than he was pressing it after being conditioned but faster than he pressed it at the end of the first extinction session. This reappearance of a conditioned response when an animal is given a rest period following extinction is called *spontaneous recovery*.

If we continued to observe Sniffy during the second extinction session, we would note that his bar-pressing rate declined more quickly during the second extinction session than it did during the first. After only a few minutes, he would once again be pressing no more often than he pressed prior to training.

To understand what's going on here, we need to recall again that in operant conditioning animals learn which behaviors produce which reinforcers in which situations. Prior to the second extinction session during which we observed spontaneous recovery, Sniffy has experienced two reinforcement contingencies. During conditioning, bar pressing produced food. During extinction, bar pressing no longer produced food. The simplest possible interpretation of spontaneous recovery is that, during the second extinction session, Sniffy presses the bar often enough to determine which reinforcement contingency is in effect now.

Schedules of Reinforcement

In extinction the food supply is completely shut off. However, what if the food supply were unreliable? When a wild rat searches for food, there is no guarantee that it will find it in the same place every time. Most of the rat's searches are based on the probability of locating food. Going to a location where there once was food and finding none would not necessarily discourage the rat from trying again at some other time.

In a similar way, consider what your reaction might be if you turned on a light switch and the light failed to come on. How you would react would likely depend on your previous experience with that light switch. If the switch had worked reliably in the past, you would very probably immediately go look for a new lightbulb. However, if you knew the switch was unreliable, you would probably spend some time

flicking it on and off before you decided that this time the problem was likely a burned-out bulb.

The technical term for a situation in which every response is reinforced is *continuous reinforcement* (*CRF*). Skinner argued that, when continuous reinforcement is interrupted, we feel as if something strange or perhaps even humorous is happening. He used visiting a house of mirrors at an amusement park as an example. When the expected visual feedback is distorted, we find that situation humorous. However, when a student who is used to getting A's suddenly earns a grade of C on a test, she feels discouraged and upset. The student will usually go to the teacher's office to complain about how the test was graded. In contrast, when a student used to getting C's receives an A, we can also see the effects of this change in feedback. In this case, if the student has been studying more than usual, she may be encouraged to continue studying harder. Alternatively, if the student who earns a higher than expected grade has been studying no more than usual, she may conclude that the course is so easy that she can afford to study even less.

Thus far, we have discussed reinforcement as something that occurs every time Sniffy performs a target behavior (CRF) or not at all (extinction). However, we could choose to reinforce only some of Sniffy's bar presses. The technical term for reinforcing some, but not all, instances of a behavior is *partial reinforcement* (*PRF*), and a rule that determines which instances of a response to reinforce is called a *schedule of reinforcement*. PRF schedules affect the temporal patterning of responses as viewed on a cumulative record. In addition, PRF schedules enhance resistance to extinction. By enhanced resistance to extinction, we mean that, if a response has been reinforced on a PRF schedule, the subject will make more responses during extinction than would be the case if the response had always been reinforced (CRF).

The comparative effects of partial and continuous reinforcement on resistance to extinction can have real-life implications. For example, suppose that you are a parent of a young child. A common difficulty with children who are about two years old is that they frequently develop a tendency to throw temper tantrums. In fact, this problem is so common that this age is frequently called the "terrible twos." How parents react to tantrums can have a profound influence on the duration of this "phase" of their child's development.

When a child has a tantrum, you can either reinforce the tantrum behavior by giving the child what he or she wants or not reinforce the behavior by letting the child kick and scream until he or she grows tired and stops. (We assume that you are the kind of sensitive person

who would never even consider punishing a child for tantrum behavior.) The best advice to parents of children who are just beginning to have tantrums is never to reinforce the behavior. If you never reinforce the behavior, your child should pass through this phase of development quickly. However, parental solicitude being what it is, many parents end up giving in to the child, especially if a tantrum occurs in public. The findings of operant conditioning suggest that if you are going to reinforce the behavior, it is better to do so consistently. That way, when the time to extinguish the behavior comes (as come it must unless you aspire to eventually becoming the parent of a tantrum-throwing adolescent), the behavior should be easier to extinguish than would be the case if you sometimes let the child scream and sometimes give the child what he or she wants.

CRF is the most efficient way to shape a new behavior quickly. But once the target behavior has been conditioned, CRF is no longer necessary. Imagine the nursery school teacher's task with a new class of children. There are so many new things the students need to learn, not only the prescribed lessons but also the social skills that will allow them to participate in the classroom. In the beginning, the children need to be reinforced as much and as often as possible for all appropriate behaviors. The teacher dispenses praise, stickers, and certificates and stamps stars on their hands. The nursery school teacher is a dispenser of reinforcers who at first must provide as close to a CRF schedule as is possible. However, this level of reinforcement is impossible to maintain, and the children are soon exposed to a PRF schedule. In first grade, children who know an answer to a question are expected to raise their hands and wait to be called on, and not every raised hand is recognized. As long as each child gets occasional recognition, the skills they have learned will not disappear because, with partial reinforcement, it is difficult to extinguish their learned behaviors.

A schedule of reinforcement is a rule for determining, in the laboratory, which responses to reinforce. In his book *Schedules of Reinforcement*, written with C. B. Ferster, Skinner describes many different possible schedules. However, all the described schedules are made of combinations of two basic "families" of schedules: *ratio schedules* and *interval schedules*.

Ratio schedules reinforce the subject for making some particular number of responses. On a fixed ratio (FR) schedule, the number of responses required is always the same. On an FR-5 schedule, the subject must make five responses for each reinforcement. This is rather like being paid for piecework, where the amount of money earned depends on the amount of work accomplished according to a prearranged pay

scale. Skinner felt that such a schedule is dangerous to the worker. Because the amount of money earned is directly proportional to the amount of work performed, piecework tends to produce high rates of output. Skinner worried that piecework might lead laborers to work to the point of exhaustion in order to maximize their income. Labor unions usually favor paying workers for the time spent working instead of the amount of work accomplished.

When we observe animals on an FR schedule in the operant chamber, the pattern of performance seen on the cumulative record depends on the size of the ratio. Small FR schedules, which require only a small number of responses for each reinforcement, produce fast, steady responding. However, the performance of an animal that is being maintained on a large FR schedule is characterized by a pause after the receipt of each reinforcement, followed by an abrupt transition to rapid, steady responding until the next reinforcement occurs. As the size of a large FR schedule is increased, the pause after the receipt of each reinforcement becomes longer. Skinner suggested that we can see something that resembles this pattern of responding in the behavior of a student who finds it difficult to start the next task after finishing a major assignment. The student's behavior is affected by the fact that a lot more work is required before the next reinforcement is obtained.

On variable ratio (VR) schedule, the value of the schedule specifies an average number of responses required to obtain reinforcement, but the exact number of responses varies from reinforcement to reinforcement. On a VR-5 schedule, the subject must make five responses on average for each reinforcement, but the exact requirement varies from reinforcement to reinforcement. VR schedules typically produce high rates of responding with no pauses. VR schedules are common. Las Vegas–style slot machines pay off on a VR schedule, as does trying to arrange a date for Saturday night or selling something on a commission basis. In all these situations, there is some chance or probability of success associated with every "response" that you make. The more often you respond, the more often you will be reinforced.

Interval schedules reinforce the subject for the first response made after a specified time interval has elapsed since the last reinforcement was received. The time period during which reinforcement is unavailable begins when the subject receives a reinforcer. The interval thus specifies a minimum amount of time that must elapse between reinforcements. On a fixed interval (FI) schedule, the interval that must elapse before another response will be reinforced is always the same. On an FI-1 minute schedule, exactly one minute must always

elapse after the receipt of one reinforcer before another response will be reinforced.

If your university or college is typical, every class period ends at a specified time. If you observe your fellow students, you will notice that their behavior changes as the end of class approaches. Early in the class period, everyone listens fairly attentively, and many students busily take notes. However, as the end of class approaches, students begin putting their notes away and preparing to leave.

On a variable interval (VI) schedule, the time interval following reinforcement that must elapse before the next response is reinforced varies from reinforcement to reinforcement. On a VI-10 second schedule, the time interval would average 10 seconds. Few, if any, real-life situations are exactly equivalent to VI scheduling. However, trying to telephone someone whose line is frequently busy is similar to reinforcement on a VI schedule. Your call won't go through until the line is free, and the line is busy for varying periods. The difference is that on a pure VI schedule, once the time interval has elapsed, the reinforcer becomes available and remains available until the subject responds, but when you are trying to call an often busy telephone number, the line is busy and free intermittently. You can miss the connection by not trying often enough.

Each of these simple schedules produces a characteristic performance from subjects maintained on the schedule long enough for their behavior to stabilize. Depending on which schedule is involved, the animal may press the bar at a steady, predictable rate, or its response rate may vary in predictable ways. However, prior to the appearance of the characteristic pattern of responding associated with the schedule, there is a period of acquisition that occurs when the animal is first placed on the schedule.

Variable Ratio (VR) and Variable Interval (VI) Schedules

Both variable ratio (VR) and variable interval (VI) schedules produce steady responding, but at different rates. VR schedules produce fast, steady responding. VI schedules produce slow, steady responding.

The difference between the performances maintained by VR and VI schedules is nicely illustrated in an experiment described by Reynolds (1975). The experiment involved two pigeons pecking at disks for food reinforcement in separate operant chambers. The design of the experiment was a *yoked design*, which means that the behavior of the first

pigeon could affect the reinforcement schedule for the other bird. In the first chamber, pigeon A's disk pecking was reinforced on a VR schedule that the experimenter had programmed. In the other, completely isolated chamber, pigeon B's disk pecking was reinforced on a VI schedule in which the values of the intervals were determined by pigeon A's behavior. Each time pigeon A received a reinforcer for completing a ratio, a reinforcer became available for pigeon B's next response.

Figure 1.1 shows hypothetical cumulative records generated by the two birds. Note that both birds respond at a nearly constant rate, but the bird on the VR schedule responds faster than the bird on the VI schedule. Although both birds' pecking behaviors are reinforced at virtually the same instant and although both always receive the same amount of reinforcement, there is a distinct difference in the rate at which they peck. This difference must somehow be due to differences in the way in which the schedules interact with the birds' pecking behaviors. There are at least two different hypotheses that try to account for this difference in response rate.

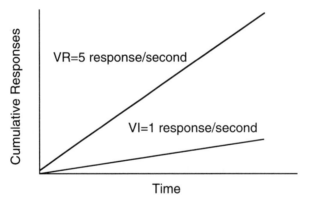

Figure 1.1

Idealized performances of two pigeons in yoked operant chambers. Both birds peck steadily. However, although both birds receive the same number of reinforcements at virtually the same instant, the VR bird makes many more responses.

One way this interaction can be viewed is in terms of *inter-response times* (*IRTs*). An inter-response time is the time that elapses between the end of one response and the beginning of the next. Each response comes at the end of the inter-response time with which it is associated. (See Figure 1.2.)

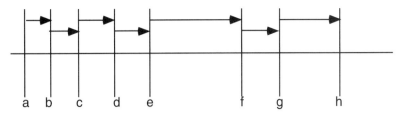

Figure 1.2

Inter-response times. Hypothetical responses a through h (vertical lines) are arranged along a time line. The arrows represent the inter-response times of the responses to which they point.

Rate of responding and the IRTs of a sequence of responses are closely related. Long IRTs are associated with slow rates, and short IRTs are associated with fast rates. A sequence of responses at a high rate will have many short IRTs and few long IRTs. The opposite is true for slow rates of responding.

Theoretically, IRTs are a response characteristic that is subject to modification by differential reinforcement. What this means is that if we reinforce mainly those responses that come at the end of short IRTs, then short IRTs should come to predominate in the performance, generating a high overall rate of responding. Similarly, if we reinforce mainly long-IRT responses, the subject should learn to make mainly long-IRT responses, thereby producing an overall slow response rate. The concept of IRTs is related to the difference in response rates maintained by VI and VR schedules because, as we shall see, VR schedules differentially reinforce short IRTs while VI schedules differentially reinforce long IRTs.

To see why this is so, let's imagine what happens when a rat that has been trained to bar press under continuous reinforcement is first switched to either a VI or a VR schedule. Animals that are being maintained on continuous reinforcement respond at a rather uneven rate. Their responses tend to occur in temporal groups called *bursts*, as illustrated in Figure 1.3. Moreover, this tendency to respond in bursts persists for a while after the animal is switched to a VI or VR schedule.

Figure 1.3

When an animal is first switched from CRF to a VI or VR schedule, it responds at an uneven rate, emitting bar presses in temporal groups called bursts. The first response in a burst has a long IRT, and the others have short IRTs. Note that more time elapses between the bursts than within them.

Note that the first response in a burst has a long IRT and the rest have short IRTs. When a VI schedule interacts with a series of bursts, the odds favor the reinforcement of the first, long-IRT responses within bursts. This is true because a VI schedule reinforces the first response that the subject makes after each interval of time during which reinforcement is unavailable has terminated. Because more time passes between the bursts than within them, the intervals during which responding is not reinforced are more likely to terminate between bursts than within them; and that fact means that more often than not the responses that are reinforced are responses that would have been the long-IRT first responses in bursts. This is what we mean when we say that VI schedules differentially reinforce long IRTs.

Now let's think about what happens when a rat is first placed on a VR schedule, which reinforces the animal for making various particular numbers of responses. Because most of the responses that the rat makes are second or later responses within bursts—responses with short IRTs—more often than not, the VR schedule will reinforce short-IRT responses. This is what we mean when we say that a VR schedule differentially reinforces short IRTs.

A second theoretical way to look at the difference in response rates maintained by VI and VR schedules is in terms of the degree of correlation between rate of response and rate of reinforcement (Figure 1.4). On a VR schedule, the rate of responding is directly proportional to the rate of reinforcement. The more rapidly the animal responds, the more frequently it is reinforced. For example, on a VR-10 schedule, an animal that makes one response per second will receive six reinforcers per minute, whereas an animal that makes two responses per second will receive 12 reinforcers per minute. Under these circumstances, a well-motivated organism should respond rapidly to get reinforced as often as possible.

However, the situation is different for an animal on a VI schedule. Although extremely low response rates can decrease the rate of reinforcement by causing long delays between the time when reinforcement becomes available and the time it is obtained, fast rates of responding are not worth the effort because reinforcers are given only for the first responses after each interval has elapsed. On a VI-10 second schedule, an animal that responds 10 times per minute will collect all six available reinforcers per minute soon after they become available. An animal that responds faster will be reinforced no more often. This difference in the correlation between response rate and reinforcement rate on VI and VR schedules is an alternative way of explaining the difference in response rates that the schedules maintain.

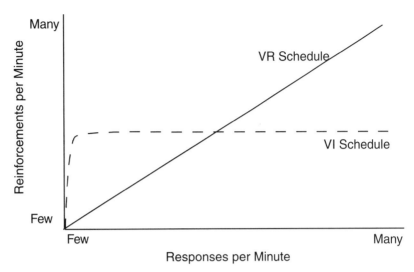

Figure 1.4

Relationship between response rate and reinforcement rate on VI and VR schedules.

Thus, we have two theoretical explanations of why animals respond faster on VR than on VI schedules, one in terms of the differential reinforcement of IRTs and the other in terms of the differential correlation between response rate and reinforcement rate. Which of these explanations is better? On the side of IRT theory are studies involving schedules designed explicitly to study the differential reinforcement of IRTs. The best known of these schedules is called the *differential reinforcement of low rates* (*drl*). A drl schedule reinforces only those responses that have IRTs greater than or equal to some specified value. For example, a drl-15 second schedule would reinforce only those responses with IRTs of 15 seconds or more. When a rat that has been trained to bar press for CRF is first placed on a drl schedule, most of its responses have IRTs that are too short to be reinforced; this lack of reinforcement produces the onset of extinction. However, as extinction takes hold and the animal's response rate declines, it will eventually make a response with an IRT long enough to be reinforced. Early in the acquisition phase of an animal's adjustment to a drl schedule, reinforcement tends to increase the response rate, which causes the animal to emit more responses with too short IRTs, which causes the extinction to set in again, which leads to the emission of another reinforceable response, and so on. The acquisition phase of adjustment to a drl schedule involves a prolonged period in which the response rate fluctuates up and down. However, gradually,

over many training sessions, the animal learns to respond slowly enough to get more and more reinforcements.

The fact that animals maintained on drl schedules improve their performance provides support to those who believe that the differential reinforcement of IRTs is the best explanation for the very different response rates maintained by VI and VR schedules. However, the fact that the acquisition phase on drl schedules is so prolonged, together with the fact that even highly trained animals make many responses with too short IRTs that cannot be reinforced, lends some credence to those who prefer to explain the different response rates maintained by VI and VR schedules in terms of differential correlations between response and reinforcement rates. However, those who favor the IRT explanation doubt that animals have the intelligence needed to perceive response-reinforcement correlations. So which explanation is better? Take your pick.

As we noted earlier, a second characteristic of the performance maintained by both VR and VI schedules is that the response rates are steady. Several factors may be involved in producing this stability. One factor involves the actual values of the intervals and ratios that make up the schedules. Response-rate stability depends on the maintenance of the intervals and ratios within certain limits. The sequence of intervals and ratios must be carefully chosen so that neither the time elapsed since the last reinforcement nor the number of responses made enables the animal to predict whether its next response will be reinforced. If there are not enough different ratio or interval values, if some of the large values are too extreme, or if the ratio or interval values come in a predictable order, the response rate maintained by the schedule will not be steady.

Once a suitable set of interval or ratio values has been chosen, another factor may enhance the degree of steadiness. Stimulus feedback from the bar-pressing performance is repeatedly associated with reinforcement, and that association may cause the feedback associated with a steady performance to become a secondary reinforcer. If that happens, the animal may begin "superstitiously" responding at a particular rate because the "feel" of responding at that rate has become a secondary reinforcer. Of course, superstitiously reinforced behavior is not confined to animals. You can see an interesting human equivalent at any bowling alley. Watch what bowlers do while the ball is rolling down the alley. Most either assume an eccentric posture or perform idiosyncratic gestures while watching the ball. Since there is no way a bowler can influence the ball's course after it leaves the hand, these postures and gestures are probably the result of the accidental association of a particular gesture or posture with the reinforcement of making a strike.

Changes in the average values of ratios and intervals in VI and VR reinforcement have characteristic effects on behavior. At almost all ratio values, VR schedules produce a very high response rate. However, beyond certain values, the range and distribution of ratios becomes critically important. Individual ratios that are too high result in abrupt pauses in responding. Pauses also occur if not enough short and medium values are included in the schedule. Such pauses of course disrupt the stable nature of the performance.

Abrupt pauses in the normally smooth and rapid performance on a VR schedule are called *strain*. Strain occurs when the average value of the ratio is increased too fast. It is possible to maintain Sniffy's bar pressing on VR schedules involving hundreds of responses per reinforcement. But the high ratio values must be approached gradually if strain, or even extinction, is to be avoided. When strain occurs, it can be eliminated by temporarily lowering the ratios.

The lengths of the intervals comprising VI schedules also influence the rate of responding. For pigeons, as the rate of reinforcement increases from zero (extinction) to about 50 per hour, response rate increases from approximately zero to about 3600 responses per hour, or one response per second. However, increases in reinforcement rates beyond about 50 per hour have little tendency to increase response rate further.

Fixed Ratio (FR) Schedules

The typical FR performance (Figure 1.5) depends on the size of the ratio—that is, on the fixed number of responses required for each reinforcement. What constitutes a small ratio depends on the organism and the effort required in making the response. For Sniffy and other rats pressing a bar, a small ratio is anything requiring up to 10 or 15 bar presses. For a pigeon pecking an illuminated disk, a small ratio is anything up to about 50. With small ratios, the performance is quite steady with no pause after each reinforcement. With large ratios, there is a pause after each reinforcement, followed by an abrupt transition to a high, stable rate until the next reinforcer is received.

The factors that produce high response rates in FR schedules are essentially the same as those in VR schedules: the differential reinforcement of short IRTs, a perfect correlation between the rate of reinforcement and the rate of responding, and the establishment of the prevailing

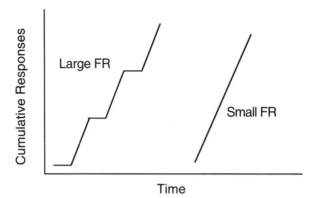

Figure 1.5

Idealized performances maintained by large and small FR schedules.

rate as a secondary reinforcer by virtue of its association with reinforcement. Thus, the only new thing that we need to explain is the pause that occurs after each reinforcement on a large FR schedule.

The post-reinforcement pause characteristic of large FR schedules is thought to be related to two factors: (1) the fact that same number of responses is required for each reinforcer, and (2) the fact that it takes some time for an animal to make the number of responses that a large FR schedule requires. What this means is that a subject that has just been reinforced on a large FR schedule "knows" that it will have to make a large number of unreinforced responses before it will be reinforced again. Most psychologists who specialize in the study of operant conditioning believe that this expectancy of a period of non-reinforced responding accounts both for the existence of post-reinforcement pauses on large FR schedules and for the fact that the pauses get longer as the FR becomes larger.

To put yourself in Sniffy's shoes, imagine yourself as a garment worker who is paid $500 for every 25 garments sewn at home. In that situation, each time you turned in a completed batch of garments and received your money, you would know that you would have to put in the time and effort required to sew another 25 garments before you received your next payment. Perhaps you would rest for a bit before starting the next batch.

Another result of the fixed-ratio scheduling of a very simple, repetitive response like bar pressing is to fuse the individual responses in the ratio into a unit consisting of a chain of responses in which each response in the unit serves as a secondary reinforcer for the previous

response. In a way, this fusion of responses into a chain of a particular length suggests that the animal can measure how many responses it makes. Support for this idea of response chaining comes from experiments with animals maintained on what is technically known as a *mixed FR schedule of reinforcement.*

A mixed FR schedule is similar to a VR schedule except that the mixed schedule has many fewer component ratio values. Let's imagine a mixed FR schedule with just two components: FR-50 and FR-150. This means that our rat has to make either 50 or 150 responses for each reinforcement. After receiving each reinforcer, an animal that has been maintained on such a schedule long enough for its behavior to stabilize pauses for the rather short time typical of a rat being maintained on a pure FR-50 schedule. Of course, if the FR-50 component is in effect for the next reinforcement, the rat receives a food pellet after making 50 responses. However, the interesting thing is what happens when the FR-150 component of the mixed schedule is in effect. After making slightly more than 50 responses, the rat pauses again, this time for the longer period typical of a rat being maintained on a pure FR-150 schedule, before completing the remaining responses required. These long mid-ratio pauses when the larger ratio component of the mixed schedule is in effect support the notion that response chaining occurs on large fixed-ratio schedules by showing that the animals can, as predicted, measure how many responses they have made.

The idea of response chaining is important because it helps to explain another characteristic of the performance on large FR schedules, the abruptness of the transition between the post-reinforcement pause and the subsequent period of responding. On large FR schedules, animals generally either respond rapidly or they don't respond at all. Response chaining explains the abrupt transition between the two response modes by hypothesizing that performing a chain of responses is functionally similar to performing a single, prolonged, effortful behavior pattern and by assuming that the animal either is engaged in the performance of the response chain or is not.

Fixed Interval (FI) Schedules

Overall, FI schedules maintain rather slow rates of responding, more or less comparable to those maintained by VI schedules. However, whereas the VI performance is steady, the typical FI performance involves a pause after the receipt of each reinforcement, followed by a gradually

accelerating response rate until the subject is responding moderately fast just before the next reinforcement is due. This typical FI performance pattern is often called the *FI scallop* (see Figure 1.6).

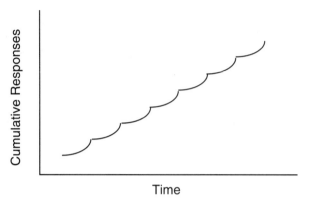

Figure 1.6

Idealized performance pattern maintained by FI schedules.

The overall slowness of the response rate maintained by FI schedules is thought to be due to the same factors that produce slow response rates on VI schedules: the differential reinforcement of long IRTs and a low correlation between response rate and reinforcement rate. Moreover, the pause following each reinforcement is thought to be due to the same factor that produces the pause on large FR schedules. Receiving a reinforcer comes to act as a signal that no further reinforcement will be forthcoming in the immediate future.

Thus the main characteristic that differentiates FI schedules is the gradualness of the transition between the period of non-responding shortly after each reinforcement is received and the moderately fast rate of responding that occurs just before the next reinforcement is due. The gradualness of this transition contrasts with the abruptness of the transition seen with FR schedules.

One reason for the difference is that the response chaining, which promotes stability of response rates during periods of responding on an FR schedule does not usually occur on an FI schedule. Response chains are thought to result from the repeated performance of exactly the same number of responses prior to the receipt of many successive reinforcers. Since FI schedules do not require subjects to make any particular number of responses and since the number of responses is in fact generally somewhat variable, response chains do not form. Thus, the reason for the abruptness of the transitions on FR schedules is ab-

sent. But the transition from non-responding to responding on FI schedules is not simply unabrupt, it is often gradual and orderly, and we need some explanation for that orderliness.

The gradually accelerating response rate often seen in subjects maintained on FI schedules is often attributed at least in part to stimulus generalization; in fact, the FI scallop can be viewed as a kind of stimulus generalization gradient. The idea is that animals have a time sense that can to some degree tell them when the next reinforcement is due. Immediately after the receipt of a reinforcer, these time-sense stimuli are very different from those previously associated with reinforcement, and the animal does not respond. However, as the interval progresses, the time-sense stimuli begin to resemble those associated with reinforcement slightly, and the animal starts responding slowly. As the interval continues to elapse, the time-sense stimuli resemble those associated with reinforcement more and more closely, and the animal responds faster and faster.

The increased tendency to respond that occurs near the end of a fixed interval is associated with a decreased tendency to do other things. If an animal can run and move about in an open area or in a wheel between pecks or bar presses, it does so less and less as the interval progresses. Also, if a second response is available and reinforced on a different schedule (for example, an FR schedule), the subject's tendency to make the second response decreases as the interval progresses, although FR performances of the second response occur regularly in the early part of each interval. We reflect this same sort of change in our own behavior when we say that we have something more important to do.

References

Kimble, G. A. (1961). *Hilgard and Marquis' Conditioning and Learning* (2nd ed.). New York: Appleton-Century-Crofts.

Reynolds, G. S. (1975). *A Primer of Operant Conditioning.* Glenview, Ill.: Scott, Foresman.

Thorndike, E. L. (1911). *Animal Intelligence: Experimental Studies.* New York: Macmillan.

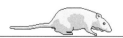

2

User's Guide

System Setup and Help Facility

Installation and setup procedures are provided at the beginning of this manual in the Quick Start section and in the Readme file that accompanies the software. Some of the following instructions also appear in the on-line help facility when the Sniffy program is running. The first screen of this help facility is shown in Figure 2.1.

Figure 2.1

Software Interface

When Sniffy is launched, your rat will begin to explore the operant chamber. As you can see in Figure 2.2, there are two windows showing the operant chamber and the cumulative record. On the back wall of the top window you can see the water spout on the left and the food hopper below a lever in the middle.

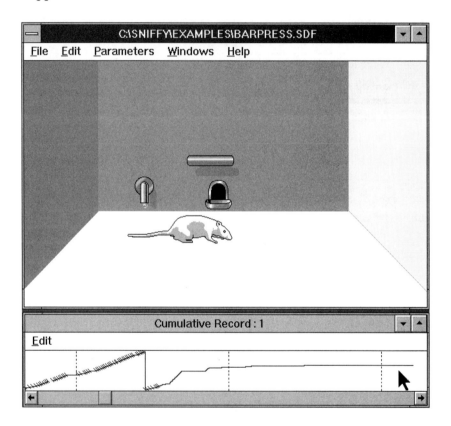

Figure 2.2

The cumulative record shown at the bottom keeps track of every bar press Sniffy makes by raising the recording pen a small amount after each press. After about 80 lever presses, the pen will reset back down to the bottom of the window. If Sniffy is reinforced on a particular bar press, a backslash is drawn just after the pen rises. In Figure 2.2 Sniffy has pressed the bar and been reinforced about 65 times before reinforcement was discontinued. After that, the cumulative record shows

another 25 or 30 bar presses with no backslashes before bar pressing becomes extinguished.

Occasionally you may inadvertently close either the operant chamber window (Sniffy's cage) or the cumulative record window. You can activate them again using the Windows menu. Up to five pages of data can be saved by the cumulative recorder, which runs for two hours. You can inspect earlier records by selecting them in the Windows menu. At the end of each two-hour record you will see the display shown in Figure 2.3. If you were to leave Sniffy running overnight or for more than 10 hours, you would be informed that the simulation has reached its time limit and been halted.

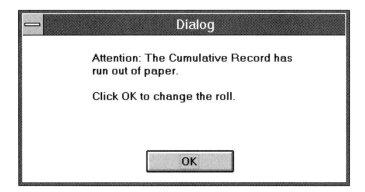

Figure 2.3

Training Sniffy the Virtual Rat

By delivering carefully timed reinforcers, you can magazine train and then shape Sniffy's behaviors. Any one of Sniffy's 15 actions can be trained to occur in specific locations within the operant chamber. However, before any behavior can be trained, the process called magazine training must be completed and a shaping procedure initiated.

To Start the Program

To start the program, open the Sniffy the Virtual Rat program group and double-click the Sniffy icon. Sniffy will begin to explore his environment after the program loads. In Figure 2.4 (page 46), we show examples of some of the actions Sniffy will exhibit. You should pull

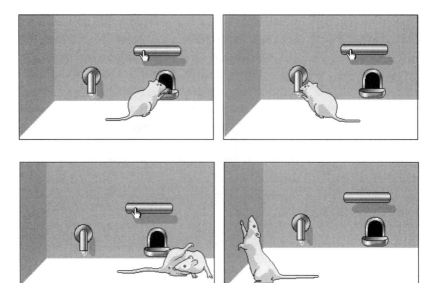

Figure 2.4

down the available menus to become familiar with the options. Sniffy will run about doing ratlike things for about 10 hours before the program terminates.

Delivering Reinforcers

To begin, you want to change Sniffy's random movements around the conditioning chamber to increase the likelihood he will go to the food magazine (hopper), where you will deliver the food reinforcements. To deliver a reinforcer manually, click on the lever on the back wall or press the spacebar on your keyboard. If the hopper has a food pellet in it, another one cannot be delivered.

Magazine Training
Wait until Sniffy is near the magazine (hopper), then click on the bar above the magazine to deliver a food pellet. It may take time for Sniffy to discover the pellet (patience is a virtue in science). After Sniffy finds and eats the pellet, immediately give him another pellet. Continue magazine training for 10 to 15 reinforcers. Your rat should be trained to approach the hopper whenever a food pellet is delivered (and he hears it drop in!). To test that your rat has been magazine trained, wait until

Sniffy is in a corner far away from the magazine, then deliver another reinforcer. If he is magazine trained, he will make his way over to the hopper and eat the cheese.

Shaping an Operant Response

Shaping allows you to speed up the learning process. It means successively changing the criteria for what behaviors deserve reinforcement. For example, consider the target behavior of Sniffy learning to bar press. To press the bar he must rear on his hind legs and come down on the bar. To shape bar pressing, begin by delivering food to the rat for simply rearing on his hind legs anywhere in the chamber (about 15 to 20 times). Then wait to reinforce only rears on the back wall, near the hopper. *Hint:* Be very vigilant. Do not miss any opportunity to reward the target behavior.

   If you are trying to train Sniffy to do a certain action in a specific location (for example, sniffing in a corner), you must start by reinforcing any action that brings him closer to that location and be prepared to reinforce all occurrences in that location.

Successive Approximation
After Sniffy is rearing often on all walls, increase the criteria for reinforcement so that the rat must not only stand on his hind legs but also do so on or near the back wall of the chamber where the bar is located. After another 10 or 15 reinforcements, deliver a cheese chunk only when he is rearing up against the back wall near the hopper. Figure 2.5 contains two examples of back-wall rearing. In the right frame, he will come down on the lever, pressing it himself if you let him. *Hint:* You may need to draw him to the back wall by occasionally delivering a pellet when he walks toward the hopper.

Figure 2.5

Continuous Reinforcement

During shaping, you should attempt to provide reinforcement every time (that is, continuously) Sniffy does what is required. The program is set by default to reinforce Sniffy's bar presses every time he presses the lever. *Hint:* Let Sniffy press the bar if it looks like he is going to. The lever mechanism makes a different sound if the hopper is already full, so do not press it before he does.

Maintaining a Behavior

Once an animal has acquired a conditioned operant response he will maintain that behavior even when he is not reinforced continuously. The Training Schedule submenu of the Parameters menu allows you to set how often Sniffy's bar presses will be followed by food. You will find that you can slowly wean Sniffy off a heavy diet of cheese and still show active bar pressing. He will learn to work harder and harder for each food pellet.

Partial Reinforcement

To change the schedule of reinforcement, select Training Schedules in the Parameters menu and set the appropriate fields. Figure 2.6 shows the dialog box for the default training schedule, called continuous reinforcement (CRF), in which all bar presses are reinforced. To stop all reinforcements, click the Extinction button.

Training Schedules

- ○ Fixed
- ○ Variable
- ● Continuous
- ○ Extinction

[1]

- ○ Seconds
- ● Responses

[Cancel] [OK]

Figure 2.6

Partial reinforcement (PRF) schedules present a food pellet after every *n* presses or on the first press after *n* seconds. PRF schedules are either fixed (where *n* is a constant—for example, for FR-10, *n* = 10) or variable (where *n* varies randomly around a constant—for example, for VI-10, *n* = 1 to 19). PRF schedules can be time-based (seconds) or behavior-based (responses). If you change to a schedule that is too lean, the animal will not maintain bar pressing. In Figure 2.7 we show the settings for a variable interval schedule, called VI-10, in which the rat is reinforced for the first bar press after a variable delay of 1 to 19 seconds.

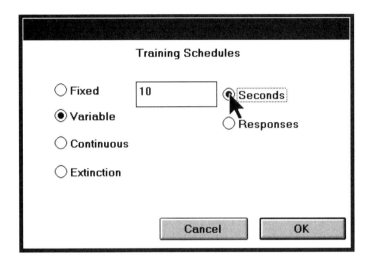

Figure 2.7

Extinction and Spontaneous Recovery

After Sniffy has been trained to bar press, you will observe the extinction and spontaneous recovery of bar pressing. The extinction procedure consists of no longer reinforcing the behavior that had previously been reinforced. As a consequence, the previously reinforced behavior will become less frequent until eventually the bar-pressing response that you conditioned will occur no more frequently than it did before conditioning. However, animals that have undergone shaping and extinction procedures will typically start bar pressing again when placed in the operant chamber after a delay period (for example, one day). This reappearance of the extinguished behavior is called spontaneous recovery.

Menu Information

The Sniffy program has a menu bar including the File, Edit, Parameters, Windows, and Help menus. The Windows menu allows you to open the operant chamber or cumulative record windows (described previously) if you inadvertently close them.

File Menu

Under File you can start a New animal, Open an experiment file (a trained animal), Save files, and Exit the application. You can also Print the cumulative record and Revert to a previously saved version of the training session.

When you quit the application by choosing the Exit command in the File menu (or whenever you open another Sniffy file), you will be warned that Sniffy will lose any acquired behaviors (see Figure 2.8). If you want to save Sniffy from such an amnesiac experience, click Cancel to negate the Exit command, choose Save As in the File menu, then specify the file name and directory you want the animal saved under.

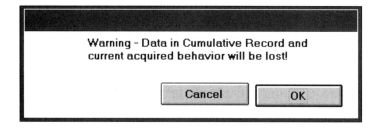

Warning - Data in Cumulative Record and current acquired behavior will be lost!

Cancel   OK

Figure 2.8

To Start with a New Sniffy

If you want to start afresh, select New in the File menu, magazine train Sniffy again, and shape his rearing and bar-pressing behavior. If you go too slowly, you may find your rat stuck on an inappropriate behavior. If you go too fast, your rat will not learn.

You can also attempt to shape alternative behaviors. Any behavior you see Sniffy performing (except drinking) can be trained to be more frequent. For instance, it is possible to train Sniffy to sniff the floor in the front right corner of the chamber if you reward sniffing in that location. (See the Advanced User's Guide in Chapter 4 for instructions on

how to use the TUVA debugging screen to monitor training.) Make sure you save your file when you are successful so that you can show off your efforts to your friends.

To Open a Sniffy File

To open a file select Open in the File menu, and find the file you want to open. Example training files are provided in the C:\sniffy\examples directory. In Figure 2.9, the Open dialog box shows some of the Sniffy files that were saved after various types of training.

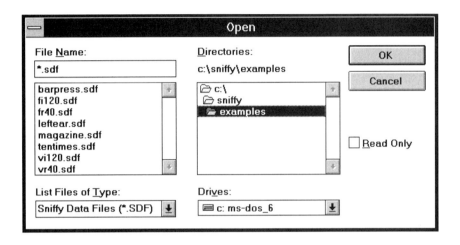

Figure 2.9

To open the files, select Open in the File menu, open the examples directory, and select the file.

magazine.sdf	magazine trained
tentimes.sdf	pressed the bar himself 10 times
barpress.sdf	trained to bar press
leftear.sdf	trained to scratch his left ear
fr40.sdf	trained on fixed-ratio schedule
vr40.sdf	trained on variable-ratio schedule
fi120.sdf	trained on fixed-interval schedule
vi120.sdf	trained on variable-interval schedule

You can also open any Sniffy files you have saved. When you open a previously saved file, Sniffy's animation rate is temporarily slowed while the cumulative record automatically scrolls to the most recent point in time. When it is first plotted, it starts at the very beginning of the file (that is, the scroll thumb is all the way to the left). Our only fix

currently is to remind the user to hand-scroll to the end of the current data as soon as the file is loaded. This will avoid the abnormal behavior associated with slow animation speeds.

To Save a Sniffy File

To save a file select Save As in the File menu, type the new file name (don't overwrite one of our example files), and save it in a directory of your choice. You can save an experiment file at any point during training so that when the file is opened again, Sniffy will have retained what he has learned to that point. Figure 2.10 shows the example of saving a partially trained rat as myfile.sdf in the C:\sniffy\examples directory.

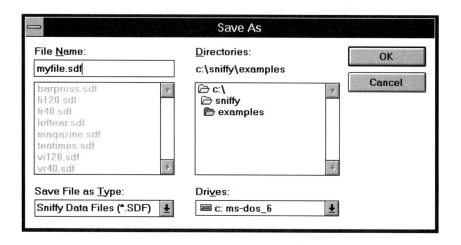

Figure 2.10

It is often wise to save your Sniffy after each stage of training so that if he fails to learn the next step, you can load the file from the previous step (using Open in the File menu) and continue rather than starting from the beginning. This highlights another benefit of simulation experiments: You can recover from mistakes without wasting too much time.

Edit Menu

The Edit menu of the cage window is currently unused. However, in the Cumulative Record window there is an Edit menu that allows you to copy bar-pressing data to a spreadsheet for detailed analyses.

In Figure 2.11 you can see a five-minute time segment during which Sniffy went from a CRF schedule to an extinction schedule. This period was selected by a point, click, and drag operation with the computer's mouse.

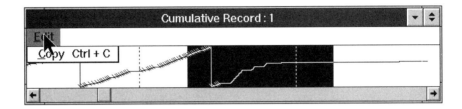

Figure 2.11

In Figure 2.12 the active window of a text editor is positioned in the upper left so that you can paste the selected data into it as a text file.

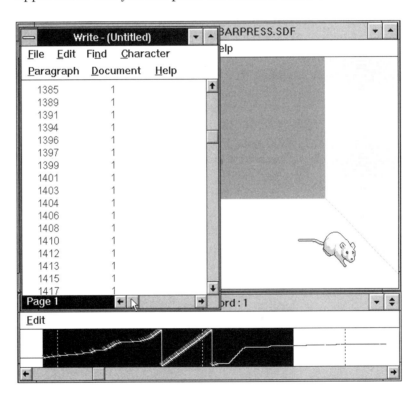

Figure 2.12

Alternatively, you could copy the data straight into your statistical software. The desired segment can be selected and, using the Edit menu of the Cumulative Record window, copied and pasted into an

open spreadsheet document reporting the time of the bar press (in 60ths of a second) and whether it was reinforced (1) or not (0). The text document shown overlaying the operant chamber in Figure 2.12 has been scrolled to the part of the file where the schedule was changed to extinction and the remaining values are 0, indicating that no reinforcements were given.

Parameters Menu

There are several submenus in the Parameters menu. You can define your own training schedules (CRF, PRF, and Extinction), study spontaneous recovery with Remove Sniffy for Time-Out, and adjust a range of default Modeling Parameters.

Training Schedules

Training Schedules are implemented after Sniffy has been conditioned to bar press. Usually, you would start with a trained rat and place him on successively leaner schedules over a period of time to wean him off food while maintaining bar-pressing behavior. The default schedule is Continuous (CRF) as shown in Figure 2.6. To set up one of the four partial reinforcement (PRF) schedules as we have done in Figure 2.7, choose Training Schedules from the Parameters menu, click either Fixed or Variable, enter the numeric value, click either Seconds (for interval) or Responses (for ratio), and click OK. To stop all reinforcements, click the Extinction button.

Remove Sniffy for Time-Out

We demonstrate spontaneous recovery by simulating the removal of Sniffy for a 24-hour period after he has undergone training and extinction of bar pressing and then placing him back in the chamber. This feature works only if conditioned bar pressing has first been trained and then extinguished. To observe spontaneous recovery, select Remove Sniffy for Time-Out in the Parameters menu, and click OK. Choose Cancel to undo that option (see Figure 2.13).

Very soon after Sniffy is reintroduced into the cage, you should observe an increase in bar-pressing behavior that extinguishes shortly thereafter. Figure 2.14 shows a cumulative record with a "click and drag" selection bar indicating when Sniffy was placed in the chamber. After about a minute, bar pressing recovered but soon extinguished

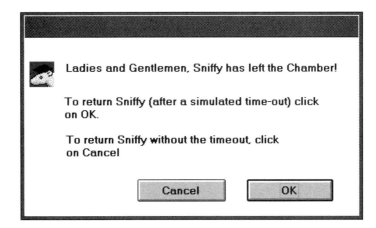

Figure 2.13

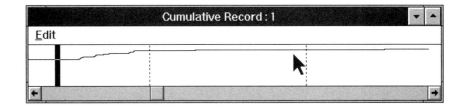

Figure 2.14

again. To date we do not attempt to simulate any of the effects of re-peated time-outs that would likely be observed in real animals.

Modeling Parameters

The Modeling Parameters menu is unavailable for use in the class-room. An advanced user can manipulate variables that affect how quickly Sniffy will learn and how quickly the action sequences are dis-played. Each variable has a five-point scale that the user sets to cus-tomize Sniffy's behavior. These are selected by clicking buttons whose values have been predetermined by the instructor.

To change these variables, the Parameters menu must be selected while the shift key is held down. Select Modeling Parameters... to make any changes. Modeling parameter variables should be set on the middle buttons (click Use Defaults) for beginning users, as shown in Figure 2.15 (page 56). The parameters are presented as ten variables with five optional settings each.

Configuration Preferences

Modeling Parameters

Magazine Training	Slow	○ ○ ◉ ○ ○	Fast
Shaping Threshold	High	○ ○ ◉ ○ ○	Low
Learning Rate	Slow	○ ○ ◉ ○ ○	Fast
Location Threshold	High	○ ○ ◉ ○ ○	Low
Deprivation	Short	○ ○ ◉ ○ ○	Long
Thirst	Seldom	○ ○ ◉ ○ ○	Often
Recovery Duration	Short	○ ○ ◉ ○ ○	Long

Intitial Seed Value: Fixed [0]   ☒ Random

Graphics Environment Parameters

Animation Governor   Slow ○ ○ ◉ ○ ○ Fast

☐ Limit Colors To: Few ○ ○ ◉ ○ ○ Lots

[Use Defaults]   [Cancel]   [OK]

Figure 2.15

The 10 parameters you can adjust are described below. The first four entries of the Modeling Parameters dialog box affect the rates and threshold values in the learning algorithms described in Chapter 4. In general, these variables should be left on the default values. For the majority of these variables, choosing a button further to the right will speed up the process, while those further left will slow down the time or increase the number of responses required for each process. You will notice that the Deprivation and Limit Colors To options are dimmed since they are not yet supported in the Windows version of Sniffy.

The 10 modeling parameters are as follows:

Magazine Training determines the speed with which you can magazine train; that is, how many minutes of training (or how many reinforcers) are required to complete magazine training.

Shaping Threshold determines the number of reinforcers required before a behavior's probability increases.

Learning Rate determines how effective a single reinforcer is in changing a behavior's probability of occurrence.

Location Threshold determines how often the reinforcer must be delivered while Sniffy is in a specific location before that sector of the chamber becomes attractive. Sniffy will learn to loiter in areas in which his behavior has been reinforced.

Deprivation simulates 24 hours of food deprivation. The program does not allow you to vary this from the default 24 hours (and thus this menu remains dimmed). We will use this menu when we have implemented satiation in the next version.

Thirst determines how often Sniffy becomes thirsty. Drinking is the only action that cannot be trained; however, it can interfere with training any other behavior.

Recovery Duration specifies how quickly spontaneous recovery and subsequent extinction will occur after Sniffy has been removed for a simulated time-out. A short duration simulates a fairly weak spontaneous recovery, whereas a long duration will produce robust recovery.

Initial Seed Value specifies a number as a fixed seed (versus a random one), creating Sniffys that will always start in the same position and follow the same sequence of behaviors until you interact by delivering a reinforcer. Thus, two computers can be started simultaneously, and the two rats will follow the same tracks. Using a random seed (the default setting) guarantees a unique Sniffy simulation each time a new Sniffy is launched.

Animation Governor controls the speed of movement (Slow to Fast) so that if your rat seems to be moving too quickly or too slowly you can correct it. Note that you can inspect the frame display rate in the TUVA screen obtained by typing `tuva` in lowercase on the keyboard while Sniffy is running. See the Rate variable in the top right corner. The ideal setting is 8 to 10 frames per second. To remove the TUVA screen type `tuva` again. See the Advanced User's Guide (Chapter 4) for details.

Limit Colors To is an option in the Macintosh version of Sniffy and has not yet been implemented in the Windows version.

Note that changes to any of the 10 modeling parameters in this preference configuration dialog box should be undertaken by advanced users only, requiring an understanding of the learning algorithms explained in Chapter 4. When the modeling parameters have been set, a sniffy.ini file is created in the C:\Windows directory to save them for the next session. In Figure 2.16 we show a set of custom settings to speed up magazine training and learning rates while slowing down the rate of animation and allowing fewer interruptions from drinking.

Configuration Preferences

Modeling Parameters

			Fast
Magazine Training	Slow	○ ○ ○ ◉ ○	Fast
Shaping Threshold	High	○ ○ ◉ ○ ○	Low
Learning Rate	Slow	○ ○ ○ ◉ ○	Fast
Location Threshold	High	○ ○ ◉ ○ ○	Low
Deprivation	Short	○ ○ ◉ ○ ○	Long
Thirst	Seldom	◉ ○ ○ ○ ○	Often
Recovery Duration	Short	○ ○ ◉ ○ ○	Long
Intitial Seed Value:	Fixed	0 ☐	Random

Graphics Environment Parameters

Animation Governor   Slow ○ ◉ ○ ○ ○ Fast

☐ Limit Colors To: Few ○ ○ ◉ ○ ○ Lots

[Use Defaults]   [Cancel]   [OK]

Figure 2.16

Windows Menu

There are two windows, one with the operant chamber and one with the Cumulative Record, as shown in Figure 2.2. You can inspect earlier records or reactivate windows you have inadvertently closed by selecting them under this menu.

Operant Chamber

The operant chamber has a water spout, a food hopper, and a bar-press lever on the back wall. The rat can wander anywhere within the four walls of the chamber. The operant chamber is divided into a number of areas called sectors, each of which can become attractive to the rat if reinforcement has been routinely given while he was in that location. Thus, not only can you train a rat to perform certain behaviors, you can also specify what area of the cage it should be done in.

TUVA Screen

There is an overlay screen for the operant chamber window that displays programming information relevant to Sniffy's learning. You can inspect the TUVA screen by typing `tuva` in lowercase on the keyboard while Sniffy is running. To remove the TUVA screen type `tuva` again. See the Advanced User's Guide (Chapter 4) for details.

Cumulative Records

The Cumulative Record window (shown below the operant chamber window) has vertical lines that represent five-minute intervals. Do not confuse these time markers with the heavy vertical lines produced when the recording pen resets. When you click on the cumulative record, you will activate that window and be able to use the scroll bar to scroll back to the beginning of the file to determine the time taken to complete various phases of training. Up to five pages of data can be saved by the cumulative recorder, which runs for two hours.

As time elapses, a line will be drawn horizontally across the screen from left to right. Every time Sniffy presses the bar, the line will move up a notch. Every time Sniffy gets a food pellet because he pressed the bar, a backslash (\) will be drawn across the line. When the line reaches the top of the record (after 80 bar presses), it will reset back down to the bottom (this is called a pen reset). If Sniffy is not bar pressing, the line will be horizontal. Up to five pages of data can be saved by the cumulative recorder; each record runs for two hours.

Help Menu

The Help menu accesses the help system stored in the C:\Sniffy\Help directory while Sniffy is running. You can start the help system without Sniffy running by opening that directory in File Manager and double-clicking Sniffy.hlp. Much of the contents of this chapter are presented in the help system. In addition, the splash screen displayed each time Sniffy is launched can be pulled up by selecting About Sniffy... in the Help menu.

3 ——— Laboratory Exercises

In the first project you will train Sniffy to press the bar on the wall of the operant chamber to obtain a food pellet. The training methods are the same ones you would use to train Sniffy to stand in the corner, scratch near the water spigot, or do any other naturally occurring behavior. They are also the same methods that would be used to train a real rat. In the second project you will study the effects of various reinforcement schedules on bar-pressing rate and their differences with respect to resistance to extinction. This exercise is designed to explore why some behaviors become persistent when they are not always followed by a positive outcome.

Project 1. Shaping an Operant Response

Training Sniffy to bar press for food is done the same way you might train your dog to fetch a stick. The purpose of this project is to demonstrate basic operant-conditioning procedures and phenomena: (1) establishing baseline behaviors, (2) magazine training, (3) shaping a behavior, (4) extinction of the conditioned behavior, and (5) spontaneous recovery. These steps are outlined in the procedures section.

We are going to use positive reinforcement to train Sniffy to press the bar more often. The positive reinforcers used to increase the frequency of the target behavior are stimuli whose presentation after the target behavior makes that behavior more likely to occur again under similar circumstances. The positive reinforcement procedure consists of waiting for a target behavior to occur and then delivering the positive reinforcer.

To be effective, *the reinforcer must be delivered to the animal immediately after the target behavior has started.* The immediacy with which the reinforcer is delivered is very important. If the reinforcer is delayed even a second or two, instead of reinforcing the target behavior, presenting the reinforcer will strengthen whatever behavior the animal was performing a second or two after it performed the target behavior.

The need for immediacy of reinforcement brings to light a problem with food as a positive reinforcer. To train Sniffy, you are going to be giving him food pellets by positioning the cursor over the bar that you are training Sniffy to press and clicking the mouse button or by pressing the spacebar on the keyboard to deliver food pellets. Unless Sniffy is very near the food hopper when the pellet is dropped, he will not find the food immediately. So what did the food pellet (the positive reinforcer) reinforce? It reinforced Sniffy for the last thing he did before he ate it, which was poking his nose into the food hopper. What we need is a positive reinforcer that can be delivered immediately after Sniffy presses the bar; that's where the procedure called *magazine training* comes in. Through magazine training, the sound of the food-delivery mechanism will become a reinforcer that can be delivered immediately after any behavior that you want to occur more often.

After magazine training, you will use a procedure called *shaping* to train Sniffy to press the lever. Shaping is the procedure used to train an animal to do often something that it normally does rarely (or not at all) by reinforcing *successive approximations* of the desired behavior. You begin by reinforcing some approximation of the target behavior that the animal performs fairly often, thereby causing that behavior to occur more frequently. Shaping works because behavior is variable. As the animal begins performing the first approximation of the target behavior more frequently, it will sooner or later perform a variant of the behavior that resembles the target behavior more closely than the first approximation. That variant then becomes the second approximation, and you require the animal to repeat that closer variant to obtain reinforcement. As the second approximation is performed more frequently, the animal will eventually emit another variant that resembles the target even more closely, and so on.

After Sniffy has been trained to bar press, you will observe the extinction and spontaneous recovery of bar pressing. The extinction procedure consists of no longer reinforcing the behavior that had previously been reinforced. As a consequence of this procedure, the previously reinforced behavior will become less frequent until eventually the bar-pressing response that you conditioned will occur no more frequently than it did before conditioning. However, animals that have

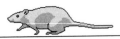

undergone shaping and extinction procedures will typically start bar pressing again when placed in the operant chamber after a delay period (for example, one day). This reappearance of the extinguished behavior is called *spontaneous recovery.*

Shaping Assignment

The following questions will need to be answered *before* you quit your Sniffy exercise. Most of them can be solved by inspecting the cumulative record and estimating times to the nearest minute by using the five-minute lines. The first three can be answered before you start training. Record your answers in Table 3.3 (page 73).

1. What was the total number of different behaviors noted?
2. What was the operant level of bar pressing (frequency per minute) before conditioning?
3. What were the four most common behaviors before training Sniffy?
4. How many minutes did it take to train Sniffy to bar press (including the 10 minutes of observation at the start)?
5. How long did it take for bar pressing to be extinguished (including the five-minute flat line)?
6. During the first minute of extinction, how many bar presses did Sniffy exhibit?
7. During the second minute of extinction, how many bar presses did Sniffy exhibit?
8. After removal for time-out, how long did it take for bar pressing to commence?
9. How long did it take for bar pressing to be extinguished again (including the five-minute flat line)?
10. During the first minute of extinction after the time-out, how many bar presses did Sniffy exhibit?
11. During the second minute of extinction after the time-out, how many bar presses did Sniffy exhibit?
12. What was the total length of time Sniffy was in the operant chamber?

Purpose

To establish and then extinguish conditioned bar pressing and observe spontaneous recovery of bar pressing after a 24-hour time-out.

Apparatus

A computer running Windows and the Sniffy 4.5 for Windows simulation software.

Procedures

When you first open the program, you will see Sniffy moving around the operant chamber (often called a Skinner box). Sniffy is hungry and therefore motivated to perform for food reinforcement. On the left side of the back wall is Sniffy's water spigot. Like a real rat in a typical operant chamber, Sniffy can have a drink of water whenever he wants one. In the center of the back wall is the bar (or lever) that you will train Sniffy to press. Below the bar is the hopper into which Sniffy's food pellets will drop.

At the bottom of the screen is the cumulative record of Sniffy's bar presses. As time elapses, a line will be drawn horizontally across the screen from left to right. Every time Sniffy presses the bar, the line will move up a notch. Every time Sniffy gets a food pellet because he pressed the bar, a backslash (\) will be drawn across the line.

When the line reaches the top of the record, it will reset back down to the bottom (this is called a pen reset). If Sniffy is not bar pressing, the line will be horizontal. Once you have trained him to press, the steepness of the line will reflect the rate of Sniffy's bar pressing. The faster he presses, the faster the line will rise. The vertical lines represent five-minute intervals. Don't confuse these time markers with the heavy vertical lines produced when the recording pen resets.

When you click on the cumulative record, you will activate that window and be able to use the scroll bar to scroll back to the beginning of the file to determine the time taken to complete various phases of training.

Step A. Behavioral Observation

The starting point in operant conditioning is observing what actions your untrained subject naturally exhibits (his baseline behaviors). Operant conditioning affects the frequency of spontaneous behaviors, so it's important to find out what your subject does before training begins.

Start with an untrained Sniffy by selecting New in the File menu. This first step documents baseline behaviors: What does a rat normally do? Observe Sniffy to become familiar with the rat's repertoire of behaviors. After watching Sniffy for a couple of minutes, making rough

notes about his behaviors, make a list of the things he does in Table 3.1 (page 71), and identify up to eight actions you see him exhibit.

Use the names of the actions as the category labels in the bottom part of Table 3.1. For the next eight minutes, keep track of Sniffy's activity minute by minute using the bottom of Table 3.1. Be precise. Don't make inferences about the behavior. Don't try to figure out what the rat likes or what he's thinking about. Just describe the behaviors objectively—for example, standing (called rearing), licking, scratching, and bar pressing.

Students could work in pairs so that one observer calls out the occurrence of behaviors in pre-established categories while the other keeps track with tick marks under those category headings in Table 3.1. The partners can make their own notes, but be warned that narrative recording is inefficient and inaccurate. Summarize your observations in Table 3.3 (page 73).

Step B. Operant Level of Bar Pressing

What is Sniffy's bar-pressing response rate before any training? This is called the *baseline rate* or *operant level* of the response that you're going to condition. Later on in this exercise (step D), you will be training Sniffy to press the bar. Thus, you need to establish how often an untrained Sniffy presses the bar per minute before you start training.

After the first 10 minutes of observation, establish the baseline frequency of bar pressing per minute. The *cumulative record* shown at the bottom of your screen shows a tick mark every time the rat was reinforced for pressing. The vertical lines indicate five-minute blocks. Therefore, count the number of ticks from the start of the cumulative record up to the second vertical line and divide by 10 to calculate the number of bar presses per minute. This value should be written in the second line of Table 3.3.

Step C. Magazine Training

Magazine training is the procedure that you are going to use to turn the sound made by the food-delivery mechanism into a secondary reinforcer for Sniffy. To start magazine training, wait until Sniffy is quite near the food hopper and then deliver a pellet of food. If he's close enough, Sniffy will find the food pellet quickly. To save time, give him several pellets of food before he wanders off. Then start delivering the food pellets when he's a little farther away from the hopper. He should orient to the hopper and grab each pellet.

When you can "call" him from any part of the chamber by operating the magazine, you know that Sniffy is magazine trained; that is, the

sound of the food-delivery mechanism has become a secondary rein-forcer. *This could take as many as 15 to 20 reinforcers.* After every five reinforcers determine whether Sniffy has been magazine trained by al-lowing him to wander away from the magazine and then delivering a food pellet. When the sound of the mechanism calls Sniffy back to the food hopper from anywhere in the operant chamber, proceed to step D.

Step D. Shaping Bar-Pressing Behavior

Shaping is the procedure used to train an animal to do often something that it normally does rarely (or not at all) by reinforcing *successive ap-proximations* of the desired behavior. To be effective, the reinforcer must be delivered to the animal *immediately* after the target behavior has started.

Keep a careful record in Table 3.2 (page 72) of the behaviors you are reinforcing. There should be a gradual shift toward the target behavior. For instance, keep track minute by minute of how often you reinforce rearing in various parts of the operant chamber. Occasionally you will reinforce other actions (such as walking toward the hopper), which you should document in the column labeled Other Actions.

As the first approximation of bar pressing, reinforce Sniffy for rear-ing up on his hind legs anywhere in the chamber. After 15 or 20 rein-forcers he should be rearing fairly often. At that point, stop reinforcing rearing at the side walls, and reinforce Sniffy only for rearing up against the back wall. Finally, gradually require him to rear closer and closer to the bar. If your patience, observational skills, and timing are average, Sniffy should be bar pressing frequently in 40 minutes or so. If you are skilled at conditioning, you can train him in half that time. The skill involved is to identify and move through the appropriate steps. If you reinforce side-wall rearing too often, Sniffy may fixate on the side walls. If you proceed too quickly, he may acquire several competing actions.

Training Tricks

1. Do not miss any chances to reinforce the target behavior. Missed opportunities will negate the effect of reinforced opportunities.
2. Move Sniffy to the back wall at least once every minute any way you can. One way of doing this is to reinforce any movements to-ward the back wall. He will learn to walk in that direction; then af-ter eating his reward you have a chance that he will rear on the back wall more often.

3. If Sniffy is rearing up near the bar, wait to let him press the bar by himself. If he presses after you have already presented the pellet, the magazine sound is different and he will not learn as quickly.

Step E. Conditioning

If your rat is not shaped after 40 minutes, ask your instructor whether you should consider starting again by selecting New from the File menu.

If you are a successful shaper, you will see Sniffy press the bar four or five times within a minute. When that happens, stop delivering reinforcers. Over the next several minutes, the response rate will climb; the cumulative record will grow steeper and steeper. When the line reaches the top of the record, it will reset down to the bottom and continue climbing back up. *Consider conditioning complete when the pen resets a second time,* as shown by the arrow in Figure 3.1.

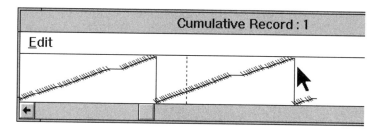

Figure 3.1

Some students may not have trained Sniffy by the end of the lab session. They can save their Sniffy at that point and continue training at another time. Or the instructor can ask them to load a trained animal file (such as barpress.sdf in the \examples directory) and continue with the next step.

Step F. Extinction: What Happens When the Food Stops?

At this point in your experiment, if your rat is bar pressing frequently, your instructor may ask you to choose Save As in the File menu and give your trained Sniffy a file name so that you have your own Sniffy file to use in the second project. (Do not save unless specifically instructed to do so.) The next step is to observe the phenomenon called extinction (which isn't nearly as fatal as it sounds) and to record bar pressing for the next two minutes to observe how quickly extinction is completed. Report your observations in Table 3.3 (page 73).

To institute extinction, choose Training Schedules in the Parameters menu, and click the Extinction button. This choice means that Sniffy will no longer be reinforced for bar pressing. Then click OK, and watch what happens over the next several minutes. The interval to use to measure extinction is the period from when Sniffy is taken off food reinforcement to the point when you can say that bar pressing has effectively stopped or at least returned to the baseline rate or operant level. In a research setting, you would establish an exact criterion, an objective definition. In the exercises, you will adopt a fairly lenient extinction criterion:

Extinction Criterion: Bar-pressing behavior is extinguished when Sniffy presses the bar fewer than three times in five minutes.

Your task is to time the period from when you instituted extinction until extinction is complete and count the number of non-reinforced bar presses during the first two minutes. You will likely observe that the rat's bar-pressing rate will decline slowly at first and then flatten out. When the cumulative record has been flat for five minutes (that is, with fewer than three bar presses), extinction is complete.

Figure 3.2 is a cumulative record during the period in which extinction was observed. We have drawn a short arrow to show the first five-minute period in which bar pressing occurred fewer than three times. The longer arrow covers the total extinction period.

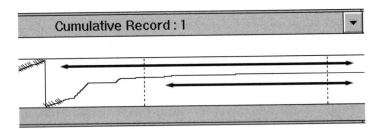

Figure 3.2

You can mark the cumulative record at the time you change schedules by pointing at the relevant section of the cumulative record, holding down your mouse button, and dragging a small distance to the right. As Sniffy's bar pressing becomes less frequent and Sniffy spends more and more of his time exploring other parts of the operant chamber, the cumulative record will begin to flatten out.

Step G. "Rest" Period

Thus far, Sniffy has been conditioned to bar press and has undergone extinction. You will now give him a night's rest and observe his behavior when you place him back in the operant chamber in the morning. To observe the effects of a time-out after extinction, select Remove Sniffy for Time-Out in the Parameters menu. This should be done only when Sniffy has been conditioned to bar press and has then undergone extinction. Click OK and proceed to step H.

Step H. Spontaneous Recovery

Measure how long it takes for bar pressing to re-emerge. Record all bar press responses for two minutes in Table 3.3. Measure the time from when Sniffy returns to the cage until bar pressing is extinguished again, using the same criterion of extinction that you used in step G.

Discussion and Interpretation

Define the following terms:

1. operant conditioning

2. operant level

3. bar press

4. magazine training

5. secondary reinforcer

6. shaping

7. extinction

8. spontaneous recovery

9. primary reinforcer

10. baseline behaviors

Short-Answer Questions

1. Shaping is a procedure that allows you to condition Sniffy to perform complex behaviors. How might you have shaped Sniffy to scratch his ear?

2. In operant conditioning you begin by magazine training your subject. Why is this step necessary? What stimulus is used in magazine training Sniffy? Why do we choose this particular stimulus?

3. Under what conditions does spontaneous recovery occur? What does spontaneous recovery tell you about extinction?

Table 3.1 Sniffy's Baseline Behaviors

Observation Notes

First Minute:

Second Minute:

Behavior Categories (write your own labels)

Minute								
3								
4								
5								
6								
7								
8								
9								
10								

Table 3.2   Reinforced Behaviors

	Rearing Frequencies			Other Actions	
Minute	Left wall	Back wall	Right wall		
1					
2					
3					
4					
5					
6					
7					
8					
9					
10					
11					
12					
13					
14					
15					
16					
17					
18					
19					
20					
21					
22					
23					
24					
25					
26					
27					
28					
29					
30					
31					
32					
33					
34					
35					
36					
37					
38					
39					
40					

Table 3.3   Shaping Assignment Summary

From Table 3.1: Steps A and B	Counts
1. Number of different behaviors:	
2. Operant level of bar pressing:	
3. Most common behaviors:	
Most common	
2nd	
3rd	
4th	
From Cumulative Record: Steps D through H	
4. Total training time:	
5. Extinction time:	
6. Bar presses in 1st minute:	
7. Bar presses in 2nd minute:	
8. Time to commence recovery:	
9. Time to extinguish again:	
10. Bar presses in 1st minute:	
11. Bar presses in 2nd minute:	
12. Total time in cumulative record:	

Project 2. Schedules of Reinforcement

The purpose of this project is to place Sniffy on a partial reinforcement schedule and observe that the schedule enhances resistance to extinction. Thus far, we have talked about reinforcement as if it were something that had to occur on every occasion. Every time Sniffy pressed the bar, he got a pellet of food. This is known as a continuous reinforcement (CRF). However, we could deliver a reinforcer after only some of Sniffy's bar presses. Reinforcing only some instances of a behavior pattern is called partial reinforcement (PRF). Before you begin, review the section on reinforcement schedules in Chapter 1.

Continuous reinforcement is the most efficient way to shape a new behavior quickly, but it is no longer necessary once the new behavior has been established. A judiciously chosen schedule of partial reinforcement can maintain a behavior indefinitely. Partial reinforcement also has the advantage of enhancing resistance to extinction.

A PRF schedule is a rule for determining which responses to reinforce. There are two basic types of schedules: ratio schedules and interval schedules.

Ratio schedules reinforce the subject for making some number of responses. On a fixed ratio (FR) schedule, the number of responses required is always the same. On an FR-5 schedule, for example, the subject must make five responses for each reinforcement. On a variable ratio (VR) schedule, the value of the schedule specifies an average number of responses that must be made, but the exact number varies from reinforcement to reinforcement. On a VR-5 schedule, for example, the behavior is reinforced for every five responses on average.

Interval schedules reinforce the subject for the first response made after a specified time interval has elapsed since the last reinforcement was received. On a fixed interval (FI) schedule, the interval that must elapse before the next response is reinforced is always the same. On an FI-10 second schedule, for example, the next response to be reinforced will be the first response that occurs after 10 seconds have elapsed following the previous reinforcement. On a variable interval (VI) schedule, the time interval following reinforcement that must elapse before the next response is reinforced varies from reinforcement to reinforcement. On a VI-10 schedule, for example, the average time that would have to expire before the animal's next bar press is reinforced would be 10 seconds. Sometimes it would occur as early as 1 or 2 seconds, other times as late as 18 or 19 seconds.

PRF Schedules Assignment

Starting with a Sniffy trained under continuous reinforcement, you will attempt to maintain bar pressing under a very large PRF schedule. To do so, you will change the PRF schedule only four times. (The details will be specified by your instructor.) After observing the acquisition of the assigned PRF schedule you will measure extinction a final time. This last step may take many minutes, during which you can complete the reports requested by your instructor.

The primary question examined in this project is as follows:

1. How long does it take for bar pressing to extinguish after a rat has been trained on a large PRF schedule (for example, VR-30 or FI-240 seconds)? How does this compare to extinction after CRF, as determined in step F of Project 1?

When you implement the partial reinforcement training procedures, you will be forced to consider two more issues:

2. When changing from a CRF to a PRF schedule, what is the largest value that will maintain bar pressing? How big a jump can you make when changing to a leaner reinforcement schedule (for example, from FR-1 to FR-20, or from VI-5 to VI-60)?
3. How lean a PRF schedule can you train Sniffy to acquire? Would Sniffy keep pressing even if there were five minutes between reinforcements—that is, FI-300 seconds? This question can only be answered empirically. Long lab periods are required if students are to explore this question seriously.

Your instructor may assign specific questions to each research group depending on the teaching objectives. In our lab, we often assign one of the four PRF schedules to each of four sections of computers. The procedures outlined here are for the group studying variable ratio schedules, but they also apply to the groups studying FR, VI, and FI schedules. The VR group will gradually increase the criterion for reinforcement to train the animal to maintain bar pressing under a very lean schedule, VR-30.

The targets for each group should be set by the instructor. Reasonable targets to aim for could be FR-60, VR-30, FI-240, VI-120 for each of the groups, respectively. Note that much leaner schedules are possible in this simulation (for example, FR-200, VR-100, FI-600, VI-300), but they require many hours of training to establish.

You may be asked to time your training sessions to determine who has the most efficient system. Most questions related to time can be solved by inspecting the cumulative record and estimating times to the nearest minute using the five-minute lines. These records can be saved as Sniffy files and printed to be handed in with the assignment. (Please do not print anything unless specifically directed to do so.)

Purpose

To train Sniffy to maintain conditioned bar pressing on a large (that is, lean) partial reinforcement schedule (such as VR-30), and then to measure time to extinction. You *should* observe that the schedule enhances resistance to extinction.

Apparatus

A computer running Windows and the Sniffy 4.5 for Windows simulation software.

Procedures

Students should document in Table 3.4 (page 82) the effects of one of the four schedule changes required during training, reporting whether the behavior extinguishes (in which case they measure how long it took the behavior to extinguish since the last schedule change) or whether the behavior was maintained. See the specific instructions on how to use Table 3.4 at the end of step B below. Occasionally, you will be asked to save the Sniffy file after certain schedules have been learned so that you will not need to start over again if your animal's bar-pressing behavior extinguishes.

Step A. Bar Pressing under CRF (Extinction Baseline)
Our aim is to compare resistance to extinction (that is, time to extinguish bar pressing) produced by partial reinforcement schedules with extinction after continuous reinforcement. If you have already carried out step F in Project 1, you can use those results as your continuous reinforcement extinction baseline and continue with the next step. To measure extinction after CRF, open a trained Sniffy file (one of your own or the barpress.sdf file provided), and let the program run for

a minute or two. Then institute extinction by choosing Training Schedules... in the Parameters menu, clicking the Extinction button, clicking OK, and watching what happens over the next several minutes. Measure the time period from when Sniffy is taken off food reinforcement to the point when the rate of bar pressing has dropped sufficiently to meet our extinction criterion:

Extinction Criterion: Bar-pressing behavior has extinguished when Sniffy presses the bar fewer than three times in five minutes.

Report your results succinctly above Table 3.4 (page 82). For example, if it took 11.5 minutes to extinguish bar pressing after CRF training, document that as CRF–EXT. Extinguished in 11.5 min.

Step B. Selecting the First PRF Schedule

You should start with a Sniffy file in which Sniffy has already been trained to bar press for continuous reinforcement. If you successfully trained Sniffy during the first project and saved the file before extinction, open that file and start it. Otherwise, you can use the barpress.sdf file included with your software package. Let Sniffy run for a minute or two under CRF; then change to the first PRF schedule. Record whether Sniffy continues bar pressing or not.

Choose a relatively small schedule to begin with. The specific value used for your first PRF schedule would have to be determined empirically. Remember that while an animal may not be able to acquire a VI-50 schedule directly after CRF training, it can be trained to maintain bar pressing on schedules well over 100 by proceeding through intermediate schedules (for example, CRF to VI-20, then VI-20 to VI-40, then VI-40 to VI-80, and so on). Establishing how much to increment the schedule at each step requires much trial and error, and you will spend some time staring at Sniffy while waiting to determine the outcome.

PRF schedules are changed using the Training Schedules dialog box from the Parameters menu. Fixed (FI and FR) schedules are chosen by clicking the Fixed button, and variable (VI and VR) schedules are chosen by clicking the Variable button. Ratio schedules are chosen by clicking the Responses button. Interval schedules are chosen by clicking the Seconds button. Schedule values in responses or seconds are specified by typing an integer up to 999 in the number-entry box.

Sniffy's behavior will be extinguished if you choose too large a value when you first place him on a PRF schedule. Bar pressing can be maintained if you start with small response or time values, increase the

values gradually, and allow the animal's behavior to stabilize at each value before moving on to the next. If Sniffy is maintaining bar pressing at a stable rate for many reinforcements, then he is said to have met the maintenance criterion. In our labs we adopt the following:

Maintenance Criterion: Sniffy has learned the new schedule if his bar-pressing behavior is maintained at a stable rate for another seven food pellets on that schedule.

This is an arbitrary criterion designed to facilitate lab completion in less than two hours. This criterion may be modified depending on the size of the PRF schedules involved. Generally, response rates begin to stabilize within 10 reinforcements, unless the cumulative record begins to flatten out. Advanced labs might explore how the training results of each schedule depend on the criteria you adopt, an important issue in any scientific endeavor.

Record the results in Table 3.4. For a single session only one of the eight panels is required per student. The table is designed to report two attempts in each of the four PRF schedules, although your instructor will decide exactly what is required of you. Specify which schedule the animal has learned and the new schedule attempted under the Schedule heading. Report whether bar pressing is maintained or extinguished under the Outcome heading. You may be asked to report the time required to meet either the maintenance criterion (seven or more reinforced bar presses) or the extinction criterion (fewer than three bar presses in the last five minutes) under the Time heading. The last heading, labeled TUVA, is to be used at your instructor's discretion. From the TUVA screen (described in Chapter 2) you can find quantitative data about the model's performance in terms of how well the new schedule has been learned and what schedule the rat "thinks" he is operating on. For example:

Schedule	Outcome	Time
CRF–VR30	Extinguished	8.5 min.
or		
CRF–VR2	Maintained	11.5 min.

Once you have a rat maintaining bar pressing on a small PRF schedule, document your results in Table 3.4 and proceed to the next step.

Step C. Increasing the Response Criteria

When Sniffy has reached the maintenance criterion, increase the schedule to the next intermediate value using the Training Schedules dialog box. Your goal is to establish as quickly as possible the target-level PRF (such as VR-30) in four successively larger schedules, starting with CRF in step B. At this point you could try, for instance, to bump the training schedule up from VR-2 to VR-30. However, this might be too large a change, which would cause Sniffy's bar pressing to extinguish, and you would need to start again. A more moderate change would be recommended. Your task is to find a set of four steps that minimizes training time. Consider the following example:

1. CRF to VR-1
2. VR-1 to VR-2 (save a file when learning is maintained)
3. VR-2 to VR-3
4. VR-3 to VR-4 (save a file when learning is maintained)

These numbers would be terribly inefficient. Sniffy's behavior should not extinguish if you use an initial value of about 5 (for either response- or time-based schedules) and subsequently increase the schedule in increments of 5 once Sniffy's behavior has stabilized at each step. This would be a sure method of training Sniffy to a large PRF schedule but not a very quick one. If you feel adventurous and try a larger-than-average step increase, it's always a good idea to save your Sniffy file before making the change.

Save your file when Sniffy has acquired the second PRF schedule, giving the file an informative name. Save it again after the fourth and final schedule has been acquired. One of the big advantages Sniffy has over a real rat is that, if you save your work, you won't have to retrain him if his behavior does extinguish during step 3 or 4. You can reload the file from step 2 and continue with more moderate schedule changes.

Document each and every schedule change in Table 3.4. For example:

Schedule	Outcome	Time
CRF–VR30	Extinguished	8.5 min.
VR1–VR2	Maintained	2.0 min.

When you have finished documenting the time to reach the maintenance criterion in the final PRF schedule and have saved your file, proceed to the next step.

Step D. Extinction after Large PRF Schedules

The final step in this lab is to measure extinction after large PRF schedules have been acquired. We will use the same methods as in step A.

To measure extinction time, wait for one more reinforcement to occur as a signal of the time you changed Sniffy to an extinction schedule (or mark the cumulative record by holding down the mouse, pointing at the current time, and dragging a bit to the right).

Institute extinction by choosing Training Schedules in the Parameters menu, clicking the Extinction button, and clicking OK. Watch what happens over the next several minutes. Measure the time period from when Sniffy received his last food reinforcement to the point that the rate of bar pressing has dropped sufficiently to meet your extinction criterion—that is, when Sniffy has pressed the bar fewer than three times in five minutes. This may take some time. Record the result—for example:

VR4–EXT.   Extinguished 14 min.

Results and Discussion

Define the following terms:

1. continuous reinforcement

2. partial reinforcement

3. fixed interval

4. variable interval

5. fixed ratio

6. variable ratio

7. maintenance criterion

8. extinction criterion

9. inter-response time

10. scalloping

Short-Answer Questions

1. You have been feeding a pigeon at your window every night for a month. Your roommate discovers this and fears that the pigeon might fly into your room. You agree to stop. To be kind, rather than abruptly stopping the pigeon's meals, you decide to stop gradually. Will this ploy work? Why or why not?

2. Partial reinforcement can be scheduled according to two basic schedules: how much time has passed since the last reinforcement or how many responses the subject has made since the last reinforcement. What are the basic differences in subjects' responses between the two schedules? What are some real-life examples of these schedules?

3. To condition a subject to perform a new operant response that you want to be resistant to extinction, you would combine continuous and partial reinforcement schedules. Briefly describe when and why you would use each of the two schedules.

Table 3.4   Record of PRF Schedules

	Fixed Ratio				Variable Ratio			
	Schedule	Outcome	Time	TUVA	Schedule	Outcome	Time	TUVA
1								
	Extinction Time				Extinction Time			
	Schedule	Outcome	Time	TUVA	Schedule	Outcome	Time	TUVA
2								
	Extinction Time				Extinction Time			

	Fixed Interval				Variable Interval			
	Schedule	Outcome	Time	TUVA	Schedule	Outcome	Time	TUVA
1								
	Extinction Time				Extinction Time			
	Schedule	Outcome	Time	TUVA	Schedule	Outcome	Time	TUVA
2								
	Extinction Time				Extinction Time			

4

Advanced User's Guide

Modeling Parameters

There are several parameters you can manipulate to explore the features of Sniffy's learning algorithms. This flexibility of the program allows instructors to customize Sniffy to suit a variety of computer platforms running Windows, a range of classroom conditions, and a range of teaching objectives. The parameters control different aspects of the simulation. You can modify the behavior of the simulation relating to the computer environment, how quickly Sniffy trains, how and when schedule effects become apparent, and how pronounced schedule effects are.

Sniffy the Virtual Rat was developed on a Macintosh platform, which afforded a number of interesting options for sophisticated users. There is a readily available resource editor called ResEdit that you can use to open the compiled, executable program and inspect the components of the software. For instance, you can modify the sequences of digitized images that animate Sniffy, the menu options, and more importantly the parameter values used by the program to implement learning and extinction under a variety of reinforcement schedules. For our Windows version we have not found a corresponding application and thus cannot provide access to the program resources other than through the Modeling Parameters menu and its associated sniffy.ini preference file.

This chapter describes how to alter the learning algorithm and other performance features. It also describes some of the variables available to Macintosh users only, since they are relevant to understanding how the software works. Read the rest of this manual carefully before trying any changes so that you understand what the effects should be. This chapter should be read once quickly for an overview and then again in detail. Please forgive us for using cognitive and anthropomorphic terms in explaining the inner workings of Sniffy's "mind"—that is, the learning algorithms.

Parameter Editing Techniques

The modeling parameters menu allows you to select one of the five default values provided for each of the 10 performance parameters. You can make these changes while Sniffy is running. Your settings are stored in the sniffy.ini preference file and will remain in place *on that computer* until the next time a parameter is changed. There is some risk that settings left over from a previous session may not be the settings you desire. Therefore, it is good policy to check the Parameters menu periodically to ensure the appropriate values are in place.

To change any of the parameters, select the Parameters menu while holding down the shift key, then select the Modeling Parameters menu. A novice user should limit modifications to the five settings provided for most of the 10 menu options shown in Sniffy's Modeling Parameters dialog box. We have used a reasonable range of default values for each of these menu options, allowing for some exploration of the learning model within the Sniffy software.

Daring users who are tempted to go beyond the options provided need to study this chapter closely and become familiar with editing procedures required to modify the sniffy.ini preference file located in the C:\Windows directory. This file stores your parameter settings, and when edited in a word processor will accept values other than the five defaults we have provided you with. This preference file is read by the Sniffy program upon launching.

The Sniffy preference file, sniffy.ini, can be inspected at the C:\Windows prompt by typing `type sniffy.ini` and pressing enter. On default settings you will see the following:

[Sniffy]
Sniffy the Virtual Rat=Copyright (c) 1996 University of Toronto.
Portions Copyright (c) 1996 DID Software
Hopper_Factor=14
Location_Threshold=10
Behaviour_Threshold=40
Thirsty=98
Tick Size=6
Slope Factor=8

Deprivation_Factor=24
Location_Recovery_Factor=5
Behaviour_Recovery_Factor=0
Limited_Display=0
Limited Depth=0
Starting Seed=0
[User]
Name=Dr. Jeff Graham
Company=Erindale College, Univ. of Toronto

You can edit the preference file in your word processor and save it as a text file in the Windows directory. In Table 4.1 we show you the range of values we have implemented as options for the variables in the preference file. You can set values between those listed to fine tune the way your Sniffy behaves. If you set a variable beyond the ranges we have used, however, we cannot guarantee the outcome.

Table 4.1 Default Modeling Parameters

Dialog Box Name	.ini File Name	L1	L2	L3	L4	L5
Magazine	Hopper_Factor	4	7	10	12	14
Location	Location_Threshold	14	12	10	7	4
Shaping	Behaviour_Threshold	60	50	40	30	20
Thirst	Thirsty	100	99	98	95	90
Animation	Tick Size	10	8	6	3	0
Learning	Slope Factor	12	10	8	6	4
Deprivation	Deprivation_Factor	—	—	24	—	—
Recovery	Location_Recovery_Factor	1	2	5	7	9
Recovery	Behaviour_Recovery_Factor	−20	−10	0	10	20
Limit Colors	Limited_Display	—	—	—	—	—
Limit Colors	Limited Depth	—	—	—	—	—
Initial Seed	Starting Seed	—	—	0	—	—

Modifiable Parameters

For the majority of the variables shown in Sniffy's Modeling Parameters dialog box, choosing a button further to the right will speed up the process, whereas choosing one further to the left will slow down the time or increase the number of responses required for each process. You will notice that the Deprivation and Limit Colors options are dimmed since they are not yet supported in the Windows version of

Sniffy. The two recovery parameters in the sniffy.ini file, Location_Recovery_Factor, and Behaviour_Recovery_Factor, are complex and in fact need to be yoked together. Thus, notice that we have only one Spontaneous Recovery variable in the Modeling Parameters window shown in Figure 4.1. We suggest you avoid tinkering with these variables in the sniffy.ini file.

Configuration Preferences

Modeling Parameters

Magazine Training	Slow	○ ○ ● ○ ○	Fast
Shaping Threshold	High	○ ○ ● ○ ○	Low
Learning Rate	Slow	○ ○ ○ ● ○	Fast
Location Threshold	High	○ ○ ● ○ ○	Low
Deprivation	Short	○ ○ ● ○ ○	Long
Thirst	Seldom	○ ● ○ ○ ○	Often
Recovery Duration	Short	○ ○ ○ ● ○	Long

Intitial Seed Value: Fixed   `123`   ☐ Random

Graphics Environment Parameters

Animation Governor   Slow ○ ○ ○ ● ○ Fast

☐ Limit Colors To: Few ○ ○ ● ○ ○ Lots

[Use Defaults]   [Cancel]   [OK]

Figure 4.1

In Figure 4.1 we used a fixed random seed so that all Sniffy files would start the same way and run identically until you interact with the software. On slower machines you may need to speed up the animation a little as we show here. In addition this configuration shows Sniffy less thirsty and slightly easier to train.

The definitions of the 10 modifiable variables are repeated below. Four of the 10 available variables are related to the learning algorithm (for example, the learning function specifies the slope, midpoint, and threshold values for behavior sequence and chamber location associations). Two are for food and water deprivation periods, and one adjusts

the duration of spontaneous recovery. The third-to-last parameter sets the starting seed value of the random number generator, and the last two affect screen display rates.

Magazine Training determines the speed with which you can magazine train; that is, how many minutes of training (or how many reinforcers) are required to complete magazine training. 100 divided by this number is the number of food pellets Sniffy requires to become magazine trained.
Practical range: 1–100

Shaping Threshold determines the number of reinforcers required before a behavior's probability increases. More technically, it is the number of associations where the midpoint on the learning curve should be. At this point the curve will reach its maximum slope.
Practical range: 0–100

Learning Rate determines how effective a single reinforcer is in changing a behavior's probability of occurrence.
Practical range: 2–16; smaller means faster learning, or a steeper slope of the learning curve.

Location Threshold determines how often the reinforcer must be delivered while Sniffy is in a specific location before that sector of the chamber becomes attractive. Sniffy will learn to loiter in areas in which his behavior has been reinforced. Sniffy needs this many associations to a sector before he will be attracted to it.
Practical range: 1–20

Deprivation simulates 24 hours of food deprivation. The program does not allow you to vary this from the default 24 hours (and thus this menu remains dimmed). We will use this menu when we have implemented satiation in the next version.

Thirst determines how often Sniffy becomes thirsty. Drinking is the only action that cannot be trained; however, it can interfere with training any other behavior.
Options: 100, 99, 98, 95, 90 (smaller is thirstier)

Recovery Duration specifies how quickly spontaneous recovery and subsequent extinction will occur after Sniffy has been removed for a simulated time-out. A short duration simulates a fairly weak spontaneous recovery, whereas a long duration will produce robust recovery. Since this is a combination of effects with two variables we suggest you stay with the five options we have provided.

Initial Seed Value specifies a number as a fixed seed (versus a random one), creating Sniffys that will always start in the same position and follow the same sequence of behaviors until you interact by delivering a reinforcer. Thus two computers can be started simultaneously, and the two rats will follow the same tracks. Using a random seed (the default setting) guarantees a unique Sniffy simulation each time a new Sniffy is launched.

Animation Governor controls the speed of movement (Slow to Fast) so that if your rat seems to be moving too quickly or too slowly you can correct it. Note that you can inspect the frame display rate in the TUVA screen by typing tuva in lowercase on the keyboard while Sniffy is running. See the Rate variable in the top right corner. The ideal setting is 8 to 10 frames per second. To remove the TUVA screen type tuva again.

Limit Colors To is an option in the Macintosh version of Sniffy and has not yet been implemented in the Windows version.

Non-Modifiable Parameters

In the following lists, the name of the variable is shown in quotation marks, followed by the default value. Most of these variables are related to the effects of the reinforcement schedule on the rate of responding. A short description is provided as well as a range of values that the Macintosh version of the software would accept. In the Windows version these variables are not modifiable.

"Max Freq Factor" / 60
   Upper limit of the learning curve.
   Practical range: 40–100

"Max Associations to Sectors" / 100
   Maximum number of associations there can be to a sector (location)
      in the chamber.
   Practical range: 50–200

"Large FR" / 20
   If evidence supports an FR schedule greater than this number, then
      pausing will be exhibited.
   Range: 10–50

"Large FR Wait Factor" / 15
Determines length of pause on large FR schedules.
This number/10.0 * FR = number of seconds to pause.
Range: 0–50

"Memory elements to Average" / 4
Sniffy records the last 10 reinforcement episodes and uses the last
four to average when guessing a new theory.
Range: 1–10

"Max Burst Time" / 3
If the last bar press before this reinforcement occurred more than this
number of seconds ago, then the rat will think he paused (and
hence the interval between presses is more important). Otherwise,
Sniffy figures that the number of presses is more important (that
is, response bursts).
Range: 0–5

"Variable Change Threshold" / 6
If Sniffy gets 6 or more changes in the last 10 reinforcement episodes,
he will assume the real schedule is variable.
Range: 1–10

"More than this and we switch to responses" / 4
If more than 4 of the last 10 reinforcements occurred during bursts,
then the rat should switch to thinking he is on a response-based
schedule.
Practical range: 0–9

"Less than this and we switch to time" / 2
If fewer than 2 of the last 10 reinforcements occurred during bursts
and not all the reinforcements came after the same number of
responses, then the rat should switch to thinking he is on an
interval-based schedule.
Practical range: 1–10

"Reduce location attraction on VI schedules" / 40
Reduce location attraction by this factor when on VI schedules.
Practical range: 1–100

"Reduce location attraction on VR schedules" / 8
Reduce location attraction by this factor when on VR schedules.
Range: 1–40

"Percentage Tolerance on VI changing to FI" / 10

The rat will switch to FI from VI if all times are greater than the last interval minus this percentage tolerance.

Range: 0–15

"Ratio Parameter"

The number of associations to decrement if a press is not reinforced.

11, 3   If the rat is on FR-10 (or less), every non-reinforced press decrements 3.

21, 2   If the rat is on FR-20 (or less), every non-reinforced press decrements 2.

Otherwise, every non-reinforced press decrements 1.

Practical range: 1 to 40 for the schedule range

2 to 5 for the decrement range

"Interval Parameters"

The number of associations to decrement if a press is not reinforced.

62, 3   If the rat is on FI-60 (or less), every non-reinforced press decrements 3.

122, 2   If the rat is on FI-120 (or less), every non-reinforced press decrements 2.

Otherwise, every non-reinforced press decrements 1.

Practical range: 1 to 360 for the schedule range

2 to 5 for the decrement range

Programmer's Debugging Screen

A programmer's debugging screen is overlaid on the operant chamber window when you type the password `tuva` in lowercase letters. The primary uses of the debugging screen are to find out how many associations Sniffy has at the lever sector and to monitor the history of his "guesses" about what schedule he is on. You can find out how often he has received reinforcements at various sectors, whether magazine training is completed, and the display rate (frames per second) of the action sequences. The debug screen shown in Figure 4.2 was taken shortly after starting with a new rat. Notice the small "crease" around the hopper. Sniffy has to be inside this circle when the food is delivered to notice it.

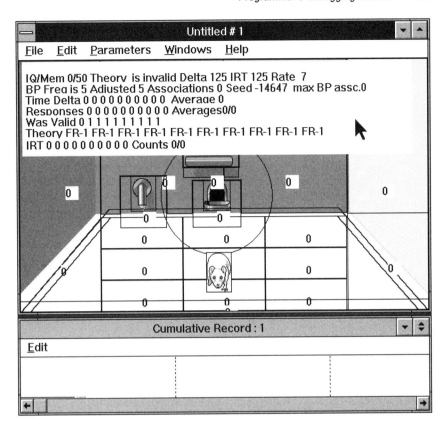

Figure 4.2

Following are definitions of the terms displayed:

IQ/Mem: Two parameters related to magazine training. If both are greater than 100, then Sniffy will approach the hopper whenever the food is delivered.

Theory Is Valid (or Invalid): Last reinforcement conditions support (or do not) support the rat's current theory of what schedule he is on.

Delta: Time in 60ths of a second since last reinforcement

IRT: Time in 60ths of a second since last bar press (inter-response time).

Rate: Screen update rate in frames per second. Note that TUVA must be turned on, off, then on again to show display rate between TUVAs.

BP Freq: Relative frequency of bar pressing. Note that all sequences start with low values (3–6), and each can increment to a maximum value. Thus, BP Freq is related to the probability of bar pressing occurring, but the actual probability at any time depends on which other sequences are playable and their current frequency values.

Adjusted: Frequencies of some actions are adjusted at the time of calculation by factors such as whether the action will bring Sniffy closer to an attractive sector.

Associations: Number of reinforcements associated with the bar sector (100 is maximum). This is also visible just below the bar.

Seed: Random seed used. Nonzero means that Sniffy will run identically on two or more machines until the trainer interacts with Sniffy, provided those machines use the same nonzero seed value.

There are also five 10-element arrays that store the last 10 reinforcement episodes used to determine what schedule Sniffy "thinks" he is on. The most recent is on the left side. The variable "memory elements to average" sets how many of the most recent events are used to 4.

Time Delta: This array stores the last 10 Deltas as defined above.

Average: The average of the most recent Deltas used as determined by "memory elements to average."

Responses: The second array stores the number of bar presses between reinforcements.

Averages A/B: A: Average of last 4 Responses.
              B: Average of last 10 Responses.

Was Valid: The third array stores whether reinforcement conditions support/do not support the rat's current theory in the last 10 reinforcements (1 is valid; 0 is invalid).

Theory: The fourth array stores Sniffy's hypothesized theory about what schedule he is on.

IRT: The fifth array stores the time since the last bar press when a bar press is reinforced.

Counts A/B: A: The number of IRTs classified as bursts according to "Max Burst Time" in the parm resource, out of "memory elements to average."
              B: The number of IRTs classified as bursts out of 10.

Location sectors have association counters that increment whenever a response is reinforced in that location. Note that small screens may have some of these on the back wall overlaid by the debug variables. The number of associations to the bar sector is available beside the variable Associations.

How Sniffy Learns

Sniffy is able to learn (and forget) actions and locations that are associated with a reward. The program does this by counting the number of rewards given while Sniffy is in each location in the operant chamber and the rewards given for the action (behavior sequence) that was being performed. This is only done if the rat is "close enough" to the hopper. "Close enough" expands as the rat becomes magazine trained. In the debug screen shown in Figure 4.2 you can see a small circle around the food hopper. Sniffy has not yet been magazine trained and will not find the food unless he wanders inside the circle.

If the reinforcement is presented when the rat is within the "close enough" circle, the circle is expanded and the rat will move toward the food. This is shown in the debug screen in Figure 4.3, while Sniffy was being magazine trained. Likewise, the circle is reduced if the rat was outside the circle when the reinforcement was presented. When the circle has expanded so that the whole operant chamber is within the

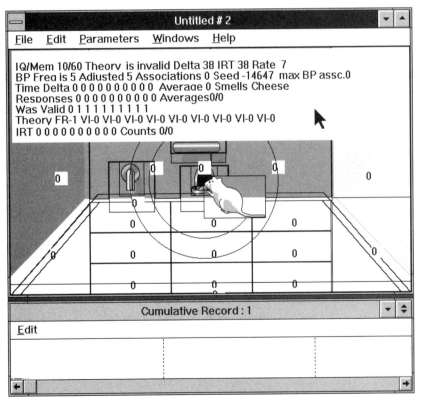

Figure 4.3

circle, the rat will always move to the food, and so he is said to be magazine trained.

Once the rat is magazine trained, he can be shaped. This shaping influences the actions he performs (behavior sequences) and the locations he frequents (sectors). The shaping of sequences and sectors are only partially independent of each other. Each is based on the number of reinforcements (associations) given when a specific action is performed in a specific location. The association will increase when the same action is again reinforced in the same location. Both can also decrease, but a sector's associations will decrease only if a behavior sequence is decreased as well. (There is one exception to this explained in the section "Decreasing Associations.")

The following sections describe behavior sequence and sector shaping (location attraction) in more detail.

Behavior Sequence Shaping

Delivering a reinforcement during an action sequence will increase the probability of that action occurring again. Each behavior sequence carries three variables that are related to shaping. Base_freq is the relative probability of this behavior sequence for an untrained rat—that is, the value the rat starts with. The variable associations is a counter of the number of pairings of this behavior sequence with the reinforcer. The base_freq is added to f(associations) to produce the value freq. This value is then used as the relative probability of this behavior sequence during selection (see "How Sniffy Selects What to Do").

The value returned by the learning function, f(associations), is calculated as follows:

```
the_sum = (–associations + behaviour_threshold)/scale_slope_factor;
the_log = (float) max_freq_factor/(1.0 + exp(the_sum));
if (the_log < 0)
    the_log = 0;
return(the_log);
```

Behaviour_threshold, scale_slope_factor, and max_freq_factor are all parameters that affect the shape of the curve. The next three figures display the learning curve for the bar press behavior sequence, showing the sum (or relative probability) on the *y*-axis, and the number of reinforcements (or associations) on the *x*-axis.

Figure 4.4 illustrates how Behaviour_threshold affects performance, showing three lines using the values 30, 40, and 50. The slope and maximum have been set to 8 and 60.

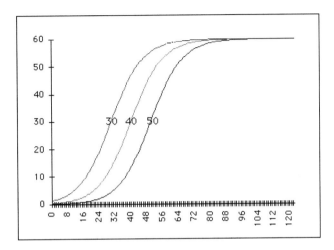

Figure 4.4

Figure 4.5 illustrates how scale_slope_factor affects performance, showing three lines using the values 4, 8, and 12. The threshold and maximum have been set to 40 and 60.

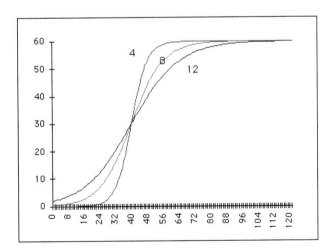

Figure 4.5

Figure 4.6 illustrates how the max_freq_factor affects performance, showing three lines using the values 40, 50, and 60. The slope and threshold values have been set to 8 and 40.

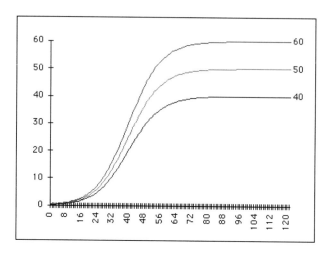

Figure 4.6

The following function is one member of the family of curves known as the logistic function (the notation ∧ means raised to the power of):

$$y = a/(1 + e^{\wedge}(-x + b)/c)$$

The default parameter values used are

a = max_freq_factor = 60	(called the same in parm)
b = behaviour_threshold = 40	(called the same in parm)
c = scale_slope_factor = 8	(called slope factor in parm)

The number of associations controls the amount of learning. As mentioned before, associations increase and decrease. Increases take place in two ways. In the simplest case, associations (both sector and behavior sequence) are increased by one when the rat is presented food. (For the remainder of this discussion, assume the rat is magazine trained.) Other cases are more complicated and are explained in the following section. The program adjusts the number of associations of behavior sequence and sector based on whether the behavior is reinforced in the routine called associate.

Decreasing Associations

A set of variables referred to as decrementing variables is used to specify how quickly extinction should occur in ratio and interval reinforcement schedules. There are two variables for these two types of schedules. Anytime the rat performs a behavior sequence and doesn't get food, he is a candidate for decrementing. Naturally, if the behavior sequence has no associations, no decrementing is performed; the same is true for sectors.

For behavior sequences with associations, the decrement is determined as shown in Table 4.2. Values in Range and Decrement Amount columns are determined from decp parameters (available in the Macintosh version using ResEdit); default values are given.

Locations are decremented the same amount, except when the rat gets no reward, when bar pressing at the hopper with bar-pressing associations = 0. This causes no behavior sequence decrementing (since associations = 0). However, the location may have associations greater than 0, and if so, they are decremented by the amount determined according to the table.

Table 4.2   Decrementing for Behavior Sequences with Associations

Decrementing rules during small PRF (less than thresholds indicated) schedules:			
Bar Press?	Expect Reward?	Max Sector Associations?	Decrement Amount
No			1
Yes	No		0
Yes	Yes	No	1
Yes	Yes	Yes	See below

Decrementing rules during large PRF schedules within ranges indicated:			
Schedule	Type	Range	Decrement Amount
Variable			1
Fixed	Interval	> 0 to < 63	3
Fixed	Interval	>= 63 to < 123	2
Fixed	Interval	>= 123	1
Fixed	Ratio	> 0 to < 10	3
Fixed	Ratio	>= 10 to < 23	2
Fixed	Ratio	>= 22	1

Increasing Associations

As mentioned before, any time reinforcement is given, behavior sequence associations increase by one. Associations will also increase during bar pressing if the rat is at the hopper and he does not expect a reward. Sniffy would not expect to get a reward if he thought he was on a schedule whose value had not been reached. For example, a rat who thinks he is on an FR-20 schedule presses the bar for the twelfth time since the last reinforcement. He would increment associations, since he does not expect to get a reward until he has pressed 20 times. Interval schedules work similarly. Variable schedules base the expectation on the value determined as the mean. So a rat on a VR-20 schedule would expect the reward after 20 bar presses and not before.

For incrementing associations, the increment for sequences and sectors is always one. Both the behavior sequence and the sector have maximum values established, beyond which associations will not increment. The maximum associations for sectors is set in the parm resource to 100, preventing the rat from accumulating "too many" associations. This is done to ensure extinction in a fixed, short time. Without the maximum, the associations would continue to build. If the rat were left on an FR-40 schedule for several hours and then put on an extinction schedule, it would take several hours for the behavior to extinguish. Because the maximum is relatively low, extinction in this case would occur in the same time (5–10 minutes) as a rat who had been on FR-40 for only 10 minutes.

How Sniffy Determines the Reinforcement Schedule

The program maintains three variables that correspond to the reinforcement schedule the rat "thinks" he is on: If Guess_Responses is true, the rat thinks he is on a ratio schedule; false implies an interval schedule. Guess_value is the "N" for the schedule. Guess_fixed is true if the rat is responding as if the schedule is fixed; false implies a variable schedule. An additional variable (theory_valid) is set to false if the rat discovers evidence that his current guess at the schedule is wrong.

Initially, the rat supposes FR-1 (continuous reinforcement). Each time the rat's behavior is reinforced with the food (that is, the food is presented and the rat is aware of it), the rat "remembers" the occur-

rence. The rat remembers the last maxMemItems occurrences (maxMemItems is currently 10); he also records the Delta time since the last reinforcement, the number of times he reared in the sector with the most number of associations (usually this will mean at the bar, but during training it can be different), and the four variables corresponding to the guess at current schedule.

The rat continues to think his theory is correct until he gets evidence otherwise. This happens when either he does not get a reward when he expected one or he gets a reward when he did not expect one. The expectation is based on his guess value for the schedule, so if he thinks he is on FI-20 and he presses the bar 25 seconds after the last reinforcement, then the rat will think his theory is incorrect. Similarly, if he presses the bar after only 15 seconds and gets a reward, he will think his theory is incorrect.

When the rat thinks his theory is incorrect, he tries to construct a new theory. To do this, he determines what the schedule type is for the current theory. The routine guess_at_reward performs this as follows:

If he thought he was on a fixed schedule,
> switch to a variable schedule only if he has changed his theory more times than the variable_change_threshold parameter

If he thought he was on a variable schedule,
> switch to a fixed schedule only if he has made no theory changes in the last maxMemItems

If he thought he was on a ratio schedule, he does this:
> If he has had less than response_burst_min reinforcements during bursts and not all his number of responses are the same
>> guess Interval Schedule with N = average of last num_to_average times
>
> otherwise
>> guess remains Ratio with N = average of last num_to_average times

If he thought he was on an interval schedule, he does this:
> If the guess was greater than the time we got it in,
>> guess remains Interval with N = average of last num_to_average times (if this average is greater than the current guess, then the current guess N value remains)
>
> If the guess was not greater than the time we got it in,
>> switch guess to responses with N = most recent number of responses if either

got more than time_burst_max reinforcements during bursts in last maxMemItems

average number of responses in last maxMemItems equals this number of responses

If neither case is met, N is average time of last num_in_average response times

The rat verifies his theory even when the theory_valid has not been set to false. There are two instances that allow the rat to switch back to a fixed schedule from a variable one:

The rat switches from VR to FR if each reinforcement has come after the same number of reinforcements.

The rat switches from VI to FI if no reinforcement has come with a Delta time less than the current Delta time (minus the "Percent Tolerance on VI changing to FI," typically 10%). (If the rat thought he was on a variable schedule, he would expect the Delta times to be evenly distributed about his mean guess. If they all are greater, minus a tolerance, it implies they are not evenly distributed, so the rat may be wrong about the variability.)

How Sniffy Selects What to Do Next

Selection of the next sequence of animation is determined by the routine findnextseqx. This routine determines where in the chamber the rat is—what sector(s) the rat is in—and whether conditions are right to perform any actions (for example, can eat if at hopper and food is in hopper).

The routine then makes two passes through the list of all behavior sequences. On the first pass, each behavior sequence is looked at and a determination is made whether the behavior sequence can be played under the current conditions. This determination is done by the routine CanPlaySeqx. If CanPlaySeqx returns true, it will also return the number of associations of the max_sector if (and only if) the behavior sequence moves the rat "closer" to the max_sector. For each of the valid behavior sequences returned by CanPlaySeqx, findnextseqx adds its frequency to a running total. The frequency is adjusted depending on a number of conditions to ensure schedule effects come out right. The adjustments are as follows:

The rat makes two checks if he is rearing at the back wall: (1) If the rat guesses he is on an FI schedule and the interval has not elapsed, then reduce frequency to frequency/amount returned from a routine called Scallop. (2) If the rat guesses he is on a large FR schedule and interval N*large_FR_wait hasn't elapsed, reduce frequency to 0.

If neither of the above is true, frequency is adjusted depending on activity (bar pressing or not) and number of associations to the location with the most associations (max sector) as follows:

If the max sector does not have more associations than the location threshold, frequency remains the same.

If the rat is not bar pressing and the max sector has more associations than the location threshold, frequency is increased by

(max_seqx_freq/base_freq) * freq * associations/total associations

If the rat is bar pressing and the max sector has more associations than the location threshold, frequency is increased by an amount that depends on whether the rat thinks he is on a fixed or a VI/VR schedule:

For fixed schedules reduce = 1.
For VR reduce = reduce_vr_parameter.
For VI reduce = reduce_vi_parameter.
Frequency is then increased by:

(max_seqx_freq * freq * associations)/(reduce * base_freq * tot_associations)

That is the amount calculated in the not-bar-pressing case divided by the factor reduce. The adjustment for variable interval schedules is necessary to reduce the overall rate of bar pressing on a VI schedule. The VR amount is necessary to ensure that the rat does not respond too rapidly when he is actually on a VI schedule. Without the reduction, a rat on a short VI schedule will respond rapidly at first. He will switch to a VR schedule because he is getting the reinforcement after a different number of responses. However, without the adjustment, he will do very little pausing, and so he will "burst" for the duration of the period. Since he will get his reinforcement during a burst, he will continue to respond as on a VR schedule (he may even switch to FR). By lowering the frequency of VR responding, pauses are introduced. The rat is more likely to get reinforcement after a pause if on VI (and after a burst if on VR), so the proper schedule is acquired.

A random number is then chosen that is between 0 and the total frequency of all the playable behavior sequences. The second pass is made, and frequencies are calculated and adjusted as before. As soon as the running total of frequency reaches the random number, the current behavior sequence is returned as the one chosen to be played. It should be noted that bar pressing refers to the behavior sequence "Rearing at Back Wall." The rat does not actually have to be at the bar for the behavior sequence to be considered bar pressing.

Index

Brooks/Cole Licensing and Warranty Agreement

This is a legal agreement between you, the program user, and Brooks/Cole Publishing Company (Publisher). **By opening the disk envelope on the inside back cover, you are agreeing to the terms of this agreement.** If you do not agree to these terms, promptly return the book and all accompanying materials.

Grant of License

Brooks/Cole Publishing Company grants you the right to use one copy of the enclosed software program ("Software") on one microcomputer at a time. You may not network the Software or otherwise use it on more than one computer at a time without obtaining a site license from the Publisher. You may not rent, lease, lend, or otherwise distribute copies of the Software to others; however, you may transfer the Software and accompanying materials on a permanent basis, provided you retain no copies and the recipient agrees to the terms of the agreement. For back-up purposes, however, you may make one copy of the Software. You may not copy any written materials that accompany the Software.

Copyright

The Software is owned by the Publisher or Author and is protected by United States copyright laws. You must treat the Software like any other copyrighted material.

Limited Warranty

The warranty for the enclosed disk is for ninety (90) days. If, during that time period, you find defects in workmanship or material, the Publisher will replace the defective item. The Publisher and the Author provide no other warranties, expressed or implied, and shall not be liable for any damages, special, indirect, incidental, consequential, or otherwise.

For warranty service, contact:

Technical Support
Brooks/Cole Publishing Company
511 Forest Lodge Road
Pacific Grove, CA 93950-5098
(800) 327-0325   FAX: (408) 373-0351
E-mail: Support@brookscole.com

BROOKS/COLE SOFTWARE REGISTRATION

Product purchased (include version number) _____

_____

If you need service, support, or information on our software, please contact our Technical Support Department.

Brooks/Cole Publishing Company
511 Forest Lodge Road
Pacific Grove, California 93950
Telephone: (800) 327-0325
FAX: (408) 373-0351
E-mail: support@brookscole.com

IMPORTANT:
Keep this portion for your records.
You will need it to receive support.

ITP™

BROOKS/COLE SOFTWARE REGISTRATION

Thank you for choosing Brooks/Cole software. To qualify for technical support and to be notified about upgrades and new products, please take a moment to complete and return this owner registration card. (This information is for internal use only.)

Name _____

❑ Student ❑ Faculty ❑ Computing Services Administrator
❑ Professional ❑ Other Administrator ❑ Personal

Department _____

Institution/Company _____

Address _____

City/State/ZIP Code _____

Telephone _____

E-mail address _____

Product purchased (include version number) _____

Date/Place of purchase _____

Equipment on which you will be using this product _____

Would you be interested in participating in an e-mail discussion group on this product? _____